The Pursuit of Dignity

New Living Alternatives for the Elderly

The Pursuit of Dignity

NEW LIVING ALTERNATIVES

FOR THE ELDERLY

BERT KRUGER SMITH

BEACON PRESS   BOSTON

Copyright © 1977 by Bert Kruger Smith

Beacon Press books are published under the auspices
of the Unitarian Universalist Association

Published simultaneously in Canada by
Fitzhenry & Whiteside Limited, Toronto

Printed in the United States of America

(hardcover) 9 8 7 6 5 4 3 2 1

Library of Congress Cataloging in Publication Data

Smith, Bert Kruger, 1915–
   The pursuit of dignity.
   Includes index.
   1. Aged—United States.   2. Aged—Dwellings—
United States.   3. Aged—Care and hygiene.   I. Title.
HQ1064.U5S584   362.6′1′0973   76–48536
ISBN 0–8070–2736–7

For Sid
Who has given sustenance
to the pursuit of life

Acknowledgments

Every acknowledgment is in itself an omission. Essentially books are written by everyone with whom a person comes in contact—persons observed, those with whom an idea is discussed, or strangers overheard. Still, specific aids are given by people involved expressly in the creation of the book.

Familial support remains paramount. The understanding of my husband, Sid, and the reinforcement from son and daughter-in-law, Sheldon and Linda Smith, and daughter and son-in-law, Sarann and John Huke, plus the enthusiasm of grandsons, Stacy and Russell Smith and Jared Huke, have been energizing.

Special and deep acknowledgment goes to the late Dr. Robert L. Sutherland, leader of the Hogg Foundation for many years and personal mentor and inspiration. Appreciation is expressed to Dr. Wayne H. Holtzman, President of the Hogg Foundation for Mental Health, The University of Texas, for encouragement and tangible allotment of time for writing. Linda Hultman is particularly thanked for her aid in typing, researching, and otherwise aiding in seeing that the book reached final form.

My thanks go out to multitudes of professional persons who were helpful. Included are Dr. Herbert Shore, Executive Director of the Dallas Home and Hospital for Jewish Aged; Dr. Hiram Friedsam, Co-Director for the Center for Studies in Aging; Allen Skidmore, Executive Director of the Texas Association of Homes for the Aging; and Dr. George Maddox, Director of the Center for the Study of Aging and Human Development at Duke University.

Contents

ix

Introduction:
Options for the Aging

In 1976, while Americans celebrated the bicentennial of an important revolution, another quiet but important revolution was taking place which is beginning to receive the attention it deserves. It is a demographic revolution in which the numbers of our older population have been growing at a very rapid rate, a rate much higher than that of the population as a whole. Our older nation has an aging population.

Some simple numbers tell an important story. The proportion of persons over 65 in the United States has doubled in this century, from 5 percent to over 10 percent. The percentage may well rise to 15 percent soon after the turn of the century. About one in three persons 65 and over is "very old" (75 and older). The "very old" are especially important because they run a high risk of debilitating illness, social isolation, poverty, and institutionalization.

Our aging population has challenged existing social arrangements in some uncomfortable ways. We simply have not planned for so many people to live so long. At birth a man has an average life expectancy of almost 69 years, a woman of more than 76 years. And if a man lives to be 65, he may expect, on the average, an additional 14 years; a woman at age 65 can expect to live an additional 18 years. Our major system of income maintenance, Social Security, is basically sound, but its cost has increased rapidly and is due to increase still more rapidly in the last quarter of this century. Our health system and our medical education were not designed to treat chronic illnesses of the kinds common to older persons. Our educational system is designed to educate merely the young, not all persons over a lifetime. Our preferences for the private automobile and for isolated suburban living serve younger people much better than older ones, although we are having some second thoughts about these preferences even for younger people.

Our first response to these demographic facts and their social implications was decidedly pessimistic. A large number of older people were visibly poor, isolated, despondent, sick, and institutionalized. Late life is a time when loss and personal trouble are common; there is no doubt about that. And death is the inevitable experience of everyone. The story of growing old in America is more complex than that, however, and should be considerably more optimistic.

Gerontological research in the last quarter of a century has taught us a great deal about adulthood and late life. We know, for example, about the various ways in which people can grow old successfully, about important continuities in lifestyle, about the importance of environment in determining behavior in late life, and, most important, about the enormous unused potential of older persons. While dying is the common outcome of living, the pathways to death are quite varied. Most older people—almost 9 out of 10—live out their lives competently in some community in contact with friends and relatives. Old people are no more alike by virtue of being old than youth are alike by being young. Old people appear in a wide variety of colors and flavors, differentiated by gender, social class, lifestyle, and, to some degree, by age.

There are important continuities in life. Older people who enjoyed their work may not prefer retirement, but they adapt well to it. Older parents who were satisfied by their role as parents tend to experience satisfactory relationships with their adult children. Active, involved middle-aged persons tend to be active, involved older persons.

The opportunities and limitations of our environment affect how we behave and how we feel, particularly so for persons whose physical and emotional reserves are declining. Instinctively we know, but need to remind ourselves, that so very often the behavior we observe among older persons is better explained by the opportunities society does or does not provide than by some mysterious process called aging. Time after time in both communities and in long-term care institutions we have seen the lives of older people literally transformed by better income, better housing, better transportation, more accessible medical care, and new learning opportunities. Which brings us to the most important point of all. Impoverished environments mask the enormous unused potential of older persons. Most people go through life with more energy, more intellectual capacity, and more emotional resources than they need most of the time. Reserve capacity diminishes in late life, but, for the most part, older people have as much capacity as they need for daily living and certainly greater capacity than society encourages them to express. It has been self-servingly convenient for us to say that our society does not need learning opportunities for older people because they are neither capable nor interested. That is demonstrable nonsense.

If older people are as varied and as capable as the facts indicate, then we have a social responsibility to increase the options for living available to our older citizens. We might take on this responsibility out of a sense of altruism and civic pride. But there is also a compelling personal reason: The lives of those currently old are a prophecy about the lives of those currently in the middle years.

Bert Kruger Smith knows all this very well. Hence she writes not only *about* the aged but also *for* the aged and the aging. She writes clearly and sensitively both about the problems late life brings and about the knowledge and actions which can aid in coping with the later years effectively. Increasing options for the old will increase the options for us all.

George L. Maddox, Director
Center for the Study of Aging
and Human Development
Duke University

What This Book Is About

This book is designed for you, whether you are young, mid-generation, or old. It may deal with problems you refuse to face, would rather not consider, or cannot tolerate. Yet you are here, reading these pages, because, whatever your age, you are part of the decision-making process of how and where the old will live.

The decision regarding alternative living patterns is difficult, often painful. Yet it must be made, for psychological reasons, sometimes for financial, and most frequently for health reasons.

We shall look at possible living arrangements for those growing old or grown old. In addition, we might consider a number of gaps in housing programs, in implementing legislation to bring about changes which would make a variety of programs possible.

Some of the possibilities will be unpleasant to face. Others might offer sensible and delightful modes of living in later years. Most will be traditional and expected. Some may be so "new style" as to raise some eyebrows.

For the young, the years may seem to be a wide road without end. Yet it is important to begin making plans early for the life views of older age. Those in the middle years are already haunted by the specter of their own forthcoming aging or by the need to plan for parents who have reached that stage in life. For them self-planning becomes imperative and immediate.

Many people in our society grow old as they have lived—with dignity and with capability. They are able to maintain themselves in their own homes throughout their lifetimes. They participate in the community and are important members of their family constellation. They maintain competence and a fair modicum of health. For them, no outside planners are needed. They are independent members of society and, though old, are still counted as productive.

Others call upon a multiple array of services and aids. And still other thousands need assistance of some kind at various times.

Everyone should know of services possible, if not for themselves, then for others who will need help during their lifetimes. Many social programs have been designed for all segments of the population, even though some groups will call upon a greater proportion of those aids than others. In programming for children, for example, many day care and educational programs geared toward enrichment of deprived children offer models for the development of children who are not deprived. Public playgrounds, libraries, recreational facilities, and health programs are beneficial to persons in all income brackets.

The same factors hold true in planning living options for older people. Day care centers, social clubs, continuing education programs, and physical fitness plans may be of paramount importance to the isolated and alienated elderly. For them socialization programs can be life rafts in a sea of loneliness. However, for all people growing older and needing new and continuing interests, the programs may offer many auxiliary supports helpful to living fully.

Therefore, this book is for you, whether you are now happily situated in that marvelous brick house in the hills or whether you have bought into a condominium where living is leisurely and with few responsibilities. The time to plan for optional living plans is now, whatever your age. As you help make decisions regarding parents or grandparents, project into future years and think of your own approaching aging.

The Pursuit of Dignity

New Living Alternatives for the Elderly

CHAPTER ONE

The Needs of the Aging: An Overview

Man is often defined by how he lives—and where. Many older people cling to living spaces which may seem inadequate because "home" may be the last bastion of reality and competence. Moving becomes far more than a physical act. It abounds with psychological meaning and impact.

The older person faced with changing living arrangements is also faced with re-ordering who he is and where his lifespace is in the world. The mental health aspects of any alteration in lifestyle become giant considerations.

Home becomes a symbol of security for the old. To stay in one's own home means to hold on to selfhood, to maintain identity. In a world which has become increasingly impersonalized, home may be the only nurturing place where a person can find himself and *be* just what he wants to be at the moment.

For the person growing older, giving up a home often symbolizes losing the last hold on independence. Yet maintaining oneself demands a certain amount of consistent competence in self-direction and self-determination. The person who lives alone has to be oriented in time, to have the strength to do the simple personal and household chores demanded of him, and to have ability to remember such duties as taking medication and turning the stove on or off.

Identity dims as he contemplates moving. The struggle to maintain self becomes too great and more demanding than strength permits. And then the person, grieving over his inability to master his destiny without external assistance, retreats into helplessness.

He is not simply giving up a home or an apartment when he moves away under the circumstances of age. Instead, he is leaving his being, a rag doll stuffed in the corner of a closet of the vacant home. He feels he will close the door on memories, on the realities of his youth, and on the person he became.

The move is not perceived as going from one location to another. Rather, it becomes a wrenching away from one life into one without personal determination. And the grieving person, shaking with the chill of loneliness, wonders about the meaning of life and of personhood. How now can he be identified? How does society regard him now that he is old?

Ministers, priests, and rabbis have defined him in terms of his highest aspirations. Educators have characterized him as a thinking, rational creature who learns about the universe and helps to solve problems. Psychologists see man in terms of his relationships; industry in terms of his work; businesses in light of his consumption of goods; farmers in regard to his intake of foods; poets with his ability to love.

We are characterized by what we do and know and feel and are. We are a macramé design, intertwined, knotted together at places, loosened from one another at others, but intricately interwoven. Untie the strands of love or work or health, and we become unraveled, individual strands of being without the design which held us together.

For many of the old in our society the strands of being are untied, and the self begins to disappear. It is said that the schizophrenic child fears looking in a mirror because he is not sure that an image will be reflected. For many old people, too, the image of self undergoes diminution or erasure as meaningful strands of living are loosened and lost.

We are a nation of "doers." What we do often characterizes who we are. One young professional woman who gave up her job in order to be with her children continued to go to professional meetings. However, she felt inadequate every time she signed a roster of attendance and was asked to fill in "Position."

Is there a "Position" for the older population? When mandatory retirement prevails, when mobility diminishes because of driving regulations, when strength must be marshaled and preserved for special tasks, are there still "positions" which are possible and satisfying for older people?

Where Are the Isolated Elderly?

How can those older people who are isolated be found? Many cannot, not without urgent and systematic searching, not without a profound sense of caring by many people.

For just a moment, let us step quietly into the life spaces of two people, hidden in the recesses of their being.

Here is one small upstairs apartment. In it the television speaks, but it is a monologue. Only a mouth. No ears to hear. And the old lady sits in front of her ever-playing television set, watching or dozing as "real" life unravels with fierceness, violence, drama, or mystery. Babies are born; men and women are unfaithful; wars are fought; people go to jail or to dances; people make love; they sing; they play music; they scream.

Like a Chinese tapestry, life itself unfolds. And the old lady remembers and forgets, forgets and recalls, in rhythm to the rocking of her chair.

The drama of life is always a pane of glass removed for many of the older people in our communities, those who live crowded in the margins of life, small spaces against the scrawled writing of the busy people—younger, more involved than they. The visible poor we know—the tots begging pennies on the common or at the border, the squatting figures with outstretched hats in the city. The obvious handicapped we recognize—those in wheelchairs, on crutches, or using walkers.

But we can easily look over, beyond, or around those who draw into the shadows of themselves, who, like chameleons, take on the color of their surroundings and fit into the shadows of their hotel rooms or small apartments. The lonely old.

The isolated old. And the ill. No crumbs are left in the corners of their lives.

Or, let's visit the old man across town. His small house is unkempt, like him—and very quiet. In the dim light slanting through the upstairs window, the old man stares at the tiny kitchen and wonders idly what canned goods in the cupboard might make some kind of supper. He is hungry but is also overcome with a kind of ennui which makes him reluctant to stir himself and try to get any food.

Everything is quiet in the late afternoon. The children outside have ceased playing in the streets. The television set isn't working, and even the birds that sometimes land on the telephone wires outside the window are no longer in sight.

Two kinds of memories crowd in on him. One has to do with summer days and boyhood. Somehow in the quick spiraling of time he sees himself on the wooden kitchen floor, barefoot, watching his mother squeeze lemons into the big flowered pitcher. Squeeze and strain; squeeze and strain. The empty lemon peelings are stacked upon one another beside the sugar canister. Sugar then and water and big hunks of ice are chipped from the large block in the ice box. He almost dozes to the remembered sound of the spoon stirring rhythmically against the glass of the pitcher. The sweet and pungent smell of lemons mingles in the air with the odor of crusty roast.

As Mother gets out the tray and glasses to take to Dad on the porch, the little boy he once was watches with a little-understood feeling of sadness at the small tower of empty lemon peelings. Just a minute ago they had been so round, so full of juice—and now Mother has gathered them up, wrapped them in paper, and thrown them into the garbage can.

The old man returns reluctantly to the little kitchen and the loneliness. Now he understands the foreboding sense of discard he had experienced as a child. The ripeness, the life-giving juices— these are gone now. Only the empty peeling remains to be discarded.

The loneliness and sense of uselessness the old man feels

can be as devastating as a physical illness. Such a person can soon fall prey to physical ills when they are compounded by loneliness.

Many older people have grown old, then poor. And they are the ones most likely to cover themselves with the cloak of isolation in order not to be seen in the shame of their discomfort. They are the ones who may sit, day after day, filtering life through news and soap operas and television dramas.

These are the people who may, with some small disaster, become instant candidates for nursing homes. They are the ones for whom some preventative attention could mean revitalization and renewal.

Isolation and Mental Impairment

The effects of isolation on the old must be viewed as we attempt to examine the present status of the elderly and the possible options which are open. If the child with serious learning disabilities could explain his feelings, he would talk of his inner sense of inadequacy, his reluctance to try anything which called for motor skills or perceptual competence. For him days may become thin shafts of sun in a field of shadows.

And if the old person whose abilities are failing could talk openly of his concerns, his words might parallel those of the child. As physical competence lessens and as organs of sight and sound and touch become impaired, the older person may well hold to the security of what he can do. He does not want to risk readjustment and change. Hostility and suspicion may be the reactions to efforts to move him into new patterns of behavior. Fear of loss and failure masks as anger, and even as he needs others, he drives them away by his behavior.

If the autistic child could speak to us, he might tell of a terror so great that his very self is in danger of dissolution. To trust, to love, to care means risk. When one loves, the beloved may damage or destroy one's self. Thus, it is thought that the mentally ill child, with some unknown hurt coursing like lifeblood within him, withdraws entirely from people. Chairs or tables, walls or beds—these do not change but remain stationary. They cannot injure. And the child turns his attention to those inanimate objects which will not alter from day to day.

If the failing older person could see himself and his needs and could verbalize them, he would mention the isolation which continues to remove him from relationships with others until he is like a small, oarless boat drifting from a familiar shore. Loved ones die; friends go also; with each loss the person seeks a place to invest his emotional energies. He often discovers that too few options exist.

Like the autistic child, he invests in "things" rather than in people. Attention goes to bodily complaints or to continual reinvestment in past memories. And the person is seen as self-absorbed rather than isolated and afraid.

The need for combating social isolation has been described by Ruth Bennett, a well-known specialist in gerontology.[1] Discussing her research regarding isolation and its effect on the older person, she confirms the relationship between isolation and low morale. What happens, Dr. Bennett finds, is that prolonged isolation in the elderly may lead to serious, and possibly irreversible, cognitive and other impairments.[2] This seems doubly sad when we recognize that the condition is often reversible through the simple therapy of friendly visiting programs and other social involvement which helps put the old person back into the heart of life.

Much of what is regarded as a sign of old age may instead be the signal of total loneliness or feelings of alienation. An aged person who is feeling the effects of such isolation may exhibit his feelings in physical or emotional symptoms.

The numbers of such lonely old people in every community are not known. Often the people are not even recognized until their behavior or health or emotional problem becomes so severe that they come to the attention of health or psychiatric agencies.

Studies of children have demonstrated that stimulation and speech are vital ingredients to a child's growth. Some recent research has shown that even newborns respond to touch and language. Without the assurance of human contact, infants can fail to develop.

Conversely, the older person who has been involved, who has held a role with status in family or community, may find life diminished as if seen through the wrong end of a telescope. And as people and activities become more and more removed, more and more remote, the older person withdraws and is increasingly unable or unwilling to function. After a period of time, immobility and ennui unite, and the older person loses many of his powers of stability as an involved human being. At the same time he ceases to try any restorative process, and the shell of isolation hardens around him.

Some parallels may well be made between the way our society treats many of its aging and the way it reacts to the terminally ill. Counselors and social scientists increasingly have reflected on the fact that surgeons, nurses, families, and friends often turn their backs on the person who will not get well. Trained in the idea of "cure," surgeons may often consider themselves failures if they are not able to achieve success through surgery. Because of their own feelings they increasingly withdraw from the incurable patient.

A knowledgeable counselor told the story of one extraordinary surgeon who had unusual empathy and feeling for all his patients. He learned to sit down with (not stand over) a bedridden patient, and he frequently gave his home telephone number to the patient, saying, "If the pain gets so bad that you are having a hard time bearing it, or if you just need someone to talk with, call me."

One of the physician's friends, hearing about this, asked the doctor about the time he would have to spend with the patients and the sleep he would lose answering late-night or early-morning telephone calls. The surgeon responded that he was rarely called but that, for the patient, the knowledge that someone aware of his plight was standing by seemed enough to help the person sustain himself through pain.

The analogy is apparent. Old persons who are in poor health or who suffer many infirmities are not going to be "cured." They will not grow better, in major ways, nor will they become younger. Therefore, we too often turn away from contact with them. Because those old people suffering from physical ailments, from isolation, are often "hidden" by their alienation, we are able to turn our backs on them, with only faint stirrings of guilt from time to time.

Despite the fact that many research findings have demonstrated that mental impairment in old people can be treated as effectively as the same impairment in the young, action on behalf of the elderly has not paralleled that for the young. Perhaps one change that is needed is in the attitudes of family members and professionals working with older people.

Psychiatrists who care for older people (and their number is not great so far) are finding that the problem of drug abuse and its effect on old people's action and possible institutional placement has to date met with little attention. Dr. Wendell R. Lipscomb stated that in his consultative practice he had encountered the iatrogenic "spaced-out" grandma syndrome. The good intentions of family doctors are often responsible for this phenomenon, according to Dr. Lipscomb. Those physicians who respond to various ailments of older people on a one-symptom, one-drug basis, without regard for possible drug interaction, thus help to provide the setting for a chemical psychosis.

In addition, patent medicines have often been abused by older people, says Dr. Lipscomb. "American's hidden drug problem persists among the aged. It is more covert, less investigated, and less written about, but in certain respects it is just as worthy of serious study as the adolescent situation," he concludes.[3]

This psychiatric interest may help undo the myth of irreversibility of mental problems in the aged which has often been the impetus for sending older people to institutions and keeping them there. Conditions which may "mask" as mental illness can include drug abuse; various physical disabilities such as congestive heart failure, kidney disease, hyperthyroidism, or others; infection accompanied by fever; depression; hearing loss and other sensory deprivation; hunger and malnutrition; and disengagement from life.

Any consideration of options in living for people growing older should take account of the mental health needs which, if alleviated, may go a long way toward helping people maintain themselves outside of 24-hour-a-day institutions. Persons who have given up on life or disengaged themselves from daily living may, with a minimum of psychiatric advice and sporadic mental health community service, be able to mobilize themselves and utilize resources within their immediate families for semi-independent living.

For the old, recovery may not be the goal. Slowing the progress of a disease, returning to partial functioning from some handicapping condition, or restoring some ability may well spell success. Anyone who has seen the patient, tedious, seemingly nonrewarding work of teachers or therapists with the seriously mentally ill child will recognize the truth of the statement that expectations have to be modified in terms of persons served.

For example, a person visiting a facility for mentally ill children watched the minute repetitive efforts made with a youngster and finally asked the teacher, "How are you able to work with so much patience, going over the same material day after day, and seeing such small results?" The teacher responded gently, "You see, when you work with these children, you learn to change your goals. You can rejoice as much over a tiny sign of attentiveness or learning as you might over a mammoth achievement in an average child."

The same principle holds true with the older population. With both physical and mental problems, therapists seem aimed toward total success and may often feel failure if they are not able to cure or restore a person.

The neglect of the mental health needs of the elderly can be documented by their disproportionate representation in the services of community health centers. In fact, one study stated that "the elderly are drastically under-represented in relation to their proportion in the population and even more importantly in relation to the higher incidence of psychopathology known to exist within this age group."[4]

Diversities Noted

While more and more people continue to grow old in our society, research about them and their needs has developed more slowly. For too long the "old" were ignored as a social phenomenon; and when they *were* regarded, they were thought of as an entity.

Now attention begins to focus on older people as a population as diverse as any other. The value systems of the various groups within the aging population are subjects of study. The group of 65 and over falls into as many patterns as persons from 35 to 65. Those facing retirement or the newly retired may be far different from the old or the very old. Within each arbitrary age division are all the diversities of human beings possible in terms of education, social status, health, and ambition.

To look at just one facet of the group, one million of the persons now elderly never went to school. Fifty percent of those currently over 65 never attended more than elementary school. One sixth of the older citizens are functionally illiterate, and only 5 percent are college graduates.[5]

Or, look at work and income patterns. Women outnumber men, with about 134 older women for every older man. Today's older women have been principally those who kept homes, reared children, and served as helpers to their husbands. They have carried into old age the same kinds of dependence which characterized their younger years. However, with the increased numbers of women in the labor force, often at top-level positions, it is likely that the next generation of older people will have many women with skills in the work arena who are competent to maintain themselves for a longer period of time in a semi-independent status. Such a shift may also mean that the poverty status of many persons who reach 65 may be changed because of pension and investment incomes which many women will have earned and Social Security payments they have garnered from their own incomes. At present only about one fifth of all aged individuals are living on income from earnings in employment. Seventy percent of such incomes are from regular retirement and Social Security.

Whether aging begins at mandatory retirement at 65 or with physical diminution at 80, the numbers of people who attain increased years are swirling upward. Taking an arbitrary figure of 65, one notes that at the turn of the century only about three million persons were 65 or older. Tripling by 1940 to nine million, the number had almost tripled again by 1975 to twenty-two million. This sevenfold increase was much higher than that of the total population, which had only tripled over the same period from seventy-six million to two hundred fifteen million.

What of the future? If the great increase in the 1970s reflected the high birth rate in families at the turn of the century, what will be the result of the lowered birth rates of the 1960s and 1970s?

Continued growth through the year 2020 is predicted. The Bureau of the Census states that there should be 24 million older people by 1980, almost 28 million by 1990, 28.8 million by 2000, 30.9 million by 2010, and 40.2 million elderly by the year 2020.[6]

The drop in the rate of growth beginning around 1990 will be the result of the Depression years. However, the "baby boom" infants who will become 65 around the year 2010 will send the numbers of older people kiting upward.

Then, after the year 2025, the decline in birth rate of the 60s and 70s will be reflected, it is thought, in a smaller older population. In summary, more and more people will reach the years of 65 and older and will swell the groups of senior persons until at least the first two decades of the twenty-first century. Although the percentage of older people to the general population will depend on many variables, including the increased life span, it is thought that by the year 2020 older people will comprise from 13 to 15 percent of the population in this country.[7] The distribution of these persons by race and sex is quite uneven. Blacks do not reach older years in the same proportion as whites; women outnumber men.

The net increase in persons 65 and over is approximately 1,400 per day or half a million per year. However, the "newcomers" differ from many of the people already categorized as old. For example, most older Americans in mid-1975 were under 75 and a third of them under 70. Almost two million people are 85 years of age or older, and more than 7,000 are 100 plus.[8]

The great dilemma remaining to be solved, then, is the means for a primarily urban, fast-moving, highly industrialized culture to plan living patterns for those whose pace is set at a slower level than that of the younger generation.

The environmental impairment problem, a fairly new phenomenon in our society, may pose one of the greatest hazards of all. Because so many of the elderly live in low-income housing in transitional or deteriorated neighborhoods, they are often subjected to danger, lack of transportation, and housing unsuitable to their needs or infirmities.

However, some options exist at every level of the aging continuum. To speak of the "older generation" as if it were an autonomous group is to do injustice to many age levels. It may be equated with talking of the learning patterns of "children" and including in the grouping infants, preschoolers, and young people up to high school age. Increasingly, with early retirement and increased life expectancy, the "young old" fall into the age group of 55 to 74, the "very old" into those 75 and above. Although many of the younger old are now responsible for the older generation, the ones in the younger age bracket are likely to be concerned with the political arena, community action, and educational opportunities.

An increasingly well-educated and healthy "young old" population will give greater attention to providing services for older people. The beginning older generation will demonstrate, through action, their concern for the parent group as well as their determination that such good facilities will be available when they reach that older age themselves.

Moving and Mental Health

The impact of adequate living arrangements upon mental health has been demonstrated among all age groups and at all socioeconomic levels. Nowhere are they more important than among the elderly.

Because decreased mobility often reduces the amount that older people can travel outside their homes, the living place becomes a life focus. For persons restricted by age infirmities, the home may be the center of practically all life activities.

Another factor which has to be considered is that "life space" for people grown old is different from the life space of a younger generation. Mobility can mean flight or change or diversity. Lack of mobility, by the same token, can be restrictive and oppressive. Old people whose life space narrows may be both more dependent on and more restricted by living arrangements which do not permit broad movement into society. They become like many of the old people living in the Virgin Islands where the lush tropical growth overtakes their homes. Because the diminished energies of the older people keep them from cutting away the brush, they become prisoners in their own homes.

The force of changes in living styles has impinged upon the older population, especially in urban areas. The multigenerational home is a rarity, and nuclear families have become the norm. Even where older persons own and have maintained a family homestead, they discover that taxes and maintenance and the inconvenience of stairways, inefficient kitchens, and basements become barriers to their mobility.

Even so, moving may be filled with trauma. The home, too old for efficiency, is crammed with memories. Photo albums and scrapbooks can go along to the new apartment or retirement hotel, but the lopsided branch on the oak tree where a tree house once stood or the rocky knoll in the backyard (once the pitcher's mound) will be lost to dim memory if others occupy the premises. A home for most people is haven and promise and friend. To be removed is to be taken away from the past.

And the old person, often knowing grief over losses, now faces a new loss. He may feel that his own being is stripped of substance and of the cover which made him unique. He becomes, to himself, a boat without anchor.

The uprooting of older people or making severe alterations

in their lifestyles may present double difficulties to persons whose competencies in some areas are diminishing. In the first place, any move presents problems. Moving away from familiar persons or surroundings is often accompanied by varying degrees of grief. This factor is true at any age.

However, in later years people often have to learn to compensate for losses in hearing or vision by maintaining a routine which will permit them to move in familiar ways and surroundings. This maneuver, which appears to be rigidity, may simply be a survival technique.

The stress of a drastic move may result in a final sense of helplessness in an older person. For many people life space has narrowed as functions have decreased. Removed from job or career, replaced in many social arenas, many people have discovered that home-bound functions too have lessened. There is neither place nor function for them to play the grandparent role. The combination of multiple losses, in the work and social arena, in the family, and in their personal accomplishments may bring feelings of depression and helplessness.

Add to those already stressful happenings the displacement of a person from familiar surroundings and places where he feels a sense of "belonging," and it is possible to precipitate disorientation and shock. Regression, depression, and other behavioral disorders often result from a change in living patterns, which may be seen by the old person as the final wrenching away of life supports which he has built throughout the years.

Because the home—whether it be a small room in a boarding house or a mansion in an urban setting—symbolizes for most people the nest of security and caring and safety, it becomes of significant importance that care be taken with the transplanting of human beings from one setting to another. It is also vital that people be kept in their own surroundings as long as they are able to exist there, even with multiple supports.

The move away from rural settings into the cities has meant several significant changes in lifestyles. For younger families it has been marked by life in smaller, individual homes or in apartments or condominiums. For the more affluent, it has meant a move to the suburbs with their broader spaces and quieter surroundings.

For those who are old a move from country to city has often meant life in small hotels, inadequate rooming houses, or apartment complexes with minimum upkeep. The move of the young affluent into the suburbs has left older populations in the inner city where often the crime rate is high and the upkeep low.

Superhighways and supermarkets provide poor settings for those who are slow drivers or slower walkers. The speed of city living may spell daily dangers for those who need to cross a street or catch a bus.

Working families often have no "remainder" of members to look after an older person who may need some help with getting dressed, getting fed, or taking medicine. The alternatives have often been: live at home or stay in an institution.

Other options exist and will be discussed in detail in this book. They are being tested throughout this country. Federal grants are going into some experiments which, if successful, can be replicated in other areas. Legislation which can provide financial help for programs such as various levels of day care may make possible the addition of such facilities in many communities. With multiple supports available, institutionalization may never need to be faced. Or, it may be postponed for many years. Alternative and supportive programs, like alternative schools for special populations of children, may become viable as the population of 65 and older moves from one in ten at present to one in six or one in eight in the year 2000.

The great differences come in the group of people 75 and over, despite the fact that many persons in that age group are independent and able to function on their own. Statistically, the group of persons 75 and over are those who need health and housing resources. With an increasing number of people living into the 80s and 90s, adjustments in living patterns and support systems become imperative. For example, in 1900, 29 percent of elderly persons were 75 years of age or over;

in 1990 about 39 percent will be in that category. Half of these will be 80 or older.[9] The truth is that most people function from adequately to well into the very late stages of life, up to the eighth or ninth decade.

Most older people, however, still live in their own homes (79 percent of elderly couples and 50 percent of both men and women lived alone or with nonrelatives in 1970). Large numbers of "frail elderly" could remain in their homes or in the households of children if enough support systems were provided to help them maintain themselves in a noninstitutional setting.

Other factors which have to be considered in thinking of ways of keeping older people "flowing" through societal waters is the diversity of people who reach their sixth, seventh, and eighth decades today compared with past generations. Just as people do not grow old at the same pace, neither do they grow old in the same way.

The supportive role of families toward older people has often been underplayed by press and other media. Studies have shown that older people, even those who are institutionalized, have frequent contact with family members. Eight percent of the men and 16 percent of the women live in homes with children.[10] Rather than abandon the old, younger families seem to keep contact and to make efforts to hold relationships to an emotionally satisfying level.

The increasing proportion of "very old" brings new dilemmas. Many of the "frail elderly," unable to maintain themselves, move in with adult children. In a mobile and urban society such living arrangements often cause tension in the family and spell disruptions in professional careers or lifestyles. The needs the old population have for health services, maintenance care, and companionship often strain the "younger" family.

The numbers of the very old also spell a new phenomenon in life styles. Increasingly, persons who have worked toward retirement and have planned for leisure find themselves responsible for very old parents. The 94-year-old man whose devoted children, 72 and 74, see him frequently, is not unique. The needs of the old for supportive living modes may be shared by their children also. Retirement hotels and nursing homes show that institutional care often becomes a family affair, with mother and daughter sharing a room or with parents and children living in the same nursing facility.

Plans for the "old" cannot be made unilaterally. Needs vary enormously according to health, mobility, age, status, and interest. Options available to one group may not be suitable for another.

Housing needs for the 65-and-over age group may be primarily directed toward finding comfortable living arrangements which are not too unwieldy or too isolated. Although many people do prefer to live in the homes they have maintained throughout many years, quite a few accept changes in living arrangements, particularly if there has been a loss of partner or a health crisis.

Living Styles for the Young Old

The growth of apartment houses and condominiums reflects the altering living style of many persons in the 65-and-over age group. High-rise apartments have been constructed for low-income older persons. These buildings are generally planned for people whose mobility may be impaired to some extent, and they are built on sites adjacent to shopping centers, restaurants, and bus lines. For older people who want it and have the means, or for those who qualify for low-income housing, such living arrangements seem to provide a workable alternative to living alone in their own homes. This group of people—in moderately good health—seem to find many positive aspects in living among their peers.

Others choose "retirement villages." These may be areas set aside and planned for the group of people in their 60s. Some of them are permanent, either small houses or apartment complexes.

For some the mobile life has much to recommend it. In sunny states like Arizona and Florida mobile home complexes with such names as "Sunny Valley" or "Senior City" flourish, particularly in winter. When cold weather begins to bite at New York, Minnesota, Washington, and other states, the mini-homes begin appearing on the highway. Many couples meet at the same centers year after year and build up a life of leisure-time activities, including square dancing, bicycle (or tricycle) riding, hiking, bowling, and swimming. Some converge in the valley areas of states like Texas and travel together. Their lightweight mobile homes provide the housing, and a group leader makes arrangements.

Some people in the "younger-old" group begin to think in terms of protective care. They are likely to go into housing providing total services from independent living in apartments to total 24-hour-a-day care. This pattern is likely to be chosen by a couple with one ill or ailing partner. Generally such facilities are maintained by exchanging such lifetime care for a substantial "buy-in" privilege and monthly charges according to the living pattern.

Some people want to be removed completely from memory of responsibility and choose to be with their own age group entirely. Others feel alienated in a box entitled "old people only."

Thus, it is possible to see that living patterns vary enormously according to the health, needs, ambitions, and preferences of the persons selecting them. The key to any possibility is *choice*.

Other Possible Supports

If people are to be maintained in communities as long as possible, the spectrum of available services will have to be far-reaching and dynamic. It is said that the earth changes even as we stand on it. So do people. No "system" can contain human beings unless that system is geared to modification and alteration. No "program" can suffice for groups of people unless that program can be tailored on short notice to new variations.

Housing is only one consideration for older people who want to remain in community settings. The needs of various people, as has been shown, may vary enormously. Physical, mental, and environmental conditions may all impinge in some fashion on the elderly.

Finances, of course, play important roles in the ability of anyone to exist in comfort. Programs to aid older people, such as Social Security, Security Supplemental Income, Medicare, and Medicaid, the many private pension or retirement funds, food stamps, and veterans benefits—all help the older person maintain a semi-independent style of life.

Personal services may come in home health programs, various nutrition efforts (transported or in congregate meal settings), or transportation programs. "Linkages" are made through telephone services of numerous kinds, from "friendly visiting" to information and referral, to medical alerts.

The ability of any person to live in his community has a close relationship to his skill in maintaining himself and his competence in obtaining those services vital to survival and well-being. Impairments may be physical (with almost half of persons over 65 limited because of some chronic condition). While the limitation may be as severe as great difficulty in simple movement, about one third reported a problem in managing stairs. Here social policy might dictate an alteration in buses, subways, housing, and buildings which could keep such people functional and independent.

Some Special Considerations

Lest it seem that home health care is a panacea and that older people who receive community services will forever remain outside of institutions, a more somber and realistic point needs to be made. As we succeed in helping people overcome serious disabilities, as we become more adept at keeping people alive after serious and life-threatening illnesses, as we save more infants who in other years would have died, we shall have an increasing population of disabled people growing old and needing institutionalization.

One recent phenomenon in our society is the larger number of seriously mentally retarded, disabled, and mentally ill people who are now old and need not only the aid their original disability might have called for but the additional supports which the problems of age have brought to them. For example, attention has been given rather recently to a new problem—that of the large population of mentally retarded persons who, instead of dying at relatively young ages, now are growing old. They bring into old age all of the needs of retarded persons plus the added needs of the elderly. Many who have suffered from severe mental problems over the years and have been hospitalized for decades grow old, too, and are doubly disadvantaged by age and mental infirmity. They will probably always need some kind of protective services along with specific aids for age-related problems. Should they go to nursing homes with previously noninstitutionalized elderly? Who decides? And how?

Our very success in saving lives becomes a problem in caring for the very old, for many people who have been crippled throughout their lifetimes will need care. Paraplegics who have been maintained and are functioning in younger years may need additional supports when they reach old years and do not have family and others to give them the full complement of services needed.

A parallel may be seen in admissions to institutions for the mentally retarded and those for the aged. With the increase in lifesaving devices for infants who might have died without heroic measures, more young people are surviving despite serious physical and mental impairments. The additional numbers of seriously disabled, coupled with the trend toward community care for those who can survive in the broader world, have meant a new population in the institutions for the retarded. More institutions are now populated by persons unable to exist without an institutional support system.

By the same token, institutions for older people are accepting a different population. Formerly, residents were physically and mentally intact old people without the financial means to maintain themselves in the community. Now, with the addition of Social Security, Old Age Survivors Disability Insurance, and new resources, many of these old people are able to maintain themselves in semi-independent fashion. One other factor enters the picture. More people are growing old; also, more old people are living to be still older. The persons entering institutions now are generally older and in poorer health than those who were residents in earlier years.

Still, it has been found that persons will generally seek out available alternatives before considering a 24-hour-a-day program. Often disabled older people will attempt to stay in their own settings even when services are not available or accessible. The recognized benefit of "home living" has served as motivation for implementation of many community programs.

We are not discussing home health aid as *opposed* to the nursing home. There is a need for both now and in the foreseeable future. The great problem is that of giving appropriate care. To institutionalize persons who could be maintained at home, with help, is a disservice. However, to keep at home those people who have need for 24-hour maintenance in a skilled facility is cruel to that population.

The vital question is how to recognize the difference in needs and how to provide appropriate care at appropriate times. It is possible that many people will need both kinds of services. For them both should be available.

In Summary

We shall consider some of the ways people faced with the prospect of having to make decisions about living patterns in older years, whether ten or thirty years from now, can maintain independent status as long as possible. This book may also serve as a guide to those currently considering alternatives for themselves or for aging parents or grandparents.

In the United States options for older people have been sparse. The private home or nursing home have too often been at the opposite ends of a continuum with no intermediate offerings in between. Although studies have shown that as many as 40 percent of older persons now in nursing homes do not need to be there on a permanent basis, alternatives have been scarce.

The magnitude of the problem is quickly recognized when one sees the percentage of old people now in nursing homes. True, only 5 percent of persons 65 and over are thus placed. However, one fourth of all people over 75 will be in nursing homes before they die.

Better home health programs could postpone or prevent institutionalization of up to 2.5 million older Americans. Even if such programs as day care, home health services, or other intermediate efforts are not highly cost effective, in some instances they can pay off in better mental health for older people who then might be maintained in familiar surroundings rather than placed in a strange institution alone.

The variety of services which can be planned is almost endless. The sponsors of such services also are wide-ranging. Housing programs can be carried out through government grants, churches, commercial groups, fraternal organizations, community services, and people at the grass roots.

Many existing housing and cooperative service programs have grown through the interest or concern of some of the groups named above. A coordinated effort to make various housing possibilities available seems in order. The thrust should come from federal policy and government assistance. With enough concerned citizen input, it may be possible to encourage demonstration programs to test various models of housing for disparate populations of older people to discover the most effective patterns which could be replicated throughout the country. Alternative models of living arrangements may, if undertaken consistently, offer a whole group of options for persons who now have to decide between home or institution without having any continuum of services on which to call.

CHAPTER TWO

Day Care for the Elderly

One of the innovative programs attempting to meet the diverse needs of the elderly is day care, which may serve people in a multitude of ways. Some, like Hildegarde Jenkins, have "private" day care centers. For Hildegarde life has not changed appreciably since Michael died, except that she has no male escort to the symphony concerts or country club dinners. But Hildegarde can buy whatever recreation she needs, and she does so via trips to Europe, catered parties at home, and afternoons at the club. When and if the time comes that Hildegarde is completely dependent on others, she will be able to "buy" her own nursing home by having round-the-clock care on her premises.

In the same town, several miles from the deep green lawns and big houses, Willie Mae Franklin grows old too, grows old like the oak in her yard, deep-rooted, rough, and ragged. For her a day care center might mean being picked up at her little house in the morning (walking carefully around the rotting spots in the steps) and going to a place where there's hot coffee, cinammon toast, a color TV, and people to laugh with.

Dolores Martinez is afraid of the strange day care center that Miss Lewis has described to her. She doesn't have a pretty dress to wear (and she knows she doesn't always smell good with just a little wash-up in the kitchen sink), and she doesn't have people to talk with. How many people will she find who speak Spanish and will visit with her when she arrives? And now that arthritis has her pinned down in a chair most of the time, how will she get from room to room in a strange place?

Who might benefit from day care? Frances Thomas, wispy as a small birch in a high wind, living in that tiny efficiency apartment above the drugstore?

Willard Green with his dirty union suit showing around his overall straps? Willard, retired from the railroad and trying to keep house in the little place he and his wife bought fifty years ago?

What about Myrtle Stover, who taught all of Central's kids their math? Genteel Myrtle, whose life savings have slowly filtered through the hour glass of time?

Or Mrs. Wilson, living with her ailing sister whose complaints drone on like an energetic insect around her head?

Then there's Maggie Rhodes, cancer-stricken but still quieting pain with laughter.

For each of these people day care services can give aid. It can be extended family. Or cook or nurse. It can be friend or chauffeur. Teacher or therapist.

Persons who have been whittled by the blade of age into a thin splinter of themselves can find within the walls of good day care centers the gifts of companionship many of them have lost.

Day care itself has many different faces. At one level the care is social, an older persons' "club" for those individuals who like to socialize, play games, travel together, and indulge in a variety of activities with people of their own age.

At another level, day care opens new options for older persons whose impairments are severe enough to make solitary living a task almost beyond ability to conquer. Transportation services, medication supervision, nursing aids all become adjuncts to the social processes which go on during the day. The staff of such centers should include therapists and nursing aides.

A third-level center becomes a day hospital, including a team of nurses and health care personnel. Post-hospital patients are accepted, as are people who are nonambulatory or chronically ill. Physical therapy, medical maintenance, health supervision become paramount in such facilities, and the "day care" becomes a euphemism for health care outside of a full-time institution.

Needs at all three levels differ for different populations. The always-poor may have recreational needs far different from upper-middle-class clients. Educational thrusts must have a semi-homogeneous group in order to be effective.

For black Willis Hendrix, who took care of dozens of yards in Midville and swung the little blonde children on the yard swings, a day care center might be a place where he can rest his swollen feet and maybe play a game or two of dominoes during the afternoon.

But Helena Backus, who used to give book reviews, cannot forgive herself for growing old and confused. She sits with a magazine on her lap, and every once in a while when the light of remembrance shines through the gray clouds of her confusion she reads a line or two.

Old Mr. Bennett, who retired from the bank when he was 70, still likes to dance. At the center he turns on the music every afternoon and waltzes every willing woman around the floor.

Tillie Davis, ill with Parkinson's disease, does well to get herself dressed in the morning. There is not enough strength left over for home maintenance (even in a one-room apartment) and for cooking. The day care center keeps her independent.

The same goes for Alice Hilliard. After her long hospitalization for a serious kidney ailment, she is minimally able to function. But, brought to the day care center, surrounded by people, fed, talked to, laughed with, she can face the evening and the night ahead.

Take Evie Harris. Still living in that two-room house with the uneven floors and the patch of rocky back yard. She might sum her life this, "Don't nothin' grow in that yard. Don't nothin' grow in this house neither. Life has shrunk down, like one of them sweaters put in hot water. Everybody gone now."

It used to be that Evie Harris could walk downtown, look

in the store windows, maybe even stop at the drugstore for some ice cream or a soda. But weight and diabetes and rising costs have halted her, and now her life is bound by the sight of the bare yard outside her kitchen window and the sometimes pictures from a seldom-working television set. She stays in her nightgown most of the day, and she doesn't remember to comb her hair.

Her family gone, her memory faltering, Evie forgets to take her medicine or fails to eat when and what she should. The Social Security check keeps up her small payments and groceries, and Evie manages to exist from marginal morning to marginal evening.

The public health nurse who saw Evie last some months ago reported then that Evie Harris could no longer live alone. Yet now Evie remains in her home; her diabetes is under better control; and her memory and general health have shown amazing alterations for the better.

The difference for Evie was day care. A center set up in her town brought Evie back into contact. A station wagon (with a nice lady who helps her with buttons or hairpins or shoelaces) comes by every day to get her. There are people waiting—people who smile a lot and act friendly. And there's toast and hot coffee and later on a real meal at a table with other people.

Besides, there are games to play and things to do and a television set that works. Someone reminds her about her medicine, and there's always a person close by who will talk a little bit and laugh sometimes, too.

Evie has begun to pay attention to her hair and dress. For her, there's something to get up for in the mornings, and she likes it that way.

Day care might mean something else to Hilda Morris. Once beautiful, once healthy, rich, once young, Hilda Morris is no longer any of these. She still maintains the façade. Somehow she manages the money and the energy to get to the beauty shop once a week. She stays in the home which she and Harvey shared for thirty years. She holds her head up and complains little.

But she is frightened. Facts elude her. They scamper like mice in a field and disappear. She cannot always remember whether or not she has eaten or turned on the oven or taken her medicine.

Hilda does not admit her feelings to her son, Milton, or to Evelyn, his wife. But she notices that they have begun talking with her in earnest about the profit she might be able to realize on the house and about how nice it would be to move somewhere where people could look after her.

But Hilda fights the thought of an institution. Not now. Not yet.

An unexpected operation precipitates the crisis. While Hilda is recovering, Milton and Evelyn put the house on the market. Hilda feels concerned. For Hilda, too, a day care center becomes refuge and delay. Her family agrees to let her try sleeping at home just so long as she spends her day at the center. The center to which Hilda goes has many people whose backgrounds are similar to hers, and she rediscovers Tillie Mathis from high school and old Bill Witsig, who used to squire most of the girls at one time or another.

Some of the bridge skills return, and the fingers which have grown non-pliable from disuse and arthritis now become a bit more supple with card dealing and playing. And some of the organizational skills return, too. Hilda, who used to manage charity balls and polio drives, begins to help again by persuading the ladies to sew dresses for dolls the Kiwanis Clubs give to little girls for Christmas.

Hilda learns to laugh again. Her appetite improves, and her memory seems to get better as good nutrition and human stimulus have an impact on her.

Both Evie Harris and Hilda Morris might well have been overlooked and lost to the rehabilitative possibilities of day care. Different though they are in color, education, and personality, they share the fact that they are among the "frail elderly" at risk in our society. It is for this population that day care centers can be of the most benefit and the one to which efforts should be directed. It has been pointed out that one out of ten old people living at home are either housebound or bedfast. This number is double that of persons in institutions. Because they are so little visible, this group is often overlooked.

Stanley McBride might not be noticed unless some percep-tive person takes time to "discover" him. The multiple losses Stanley endured over a one-year period—retirement from his position as marketing head of a big corporation, long-time illness of his wife, Martha, and finally Martha's death—brought people to the apartment. They came with flowers and kind words and casseroles. They came while Martha was ill, and they visited after she died. And then they ceased coming, and Stanley stopped going out.

Where would he go anyway? The illness had drained the bank account. The office was closed to him. The kids lived two thousand miles away, and nobody seemed anxious to have a tired old man around.

Stanley tried a few times to get in touch with some of their friends, but the too-quick replies of "Stanley, we're going to have to get together soon. But not this weekend. Some friends from Canada are stopping in for several nights, and we're all booked up."

The courage which had kept Stanley standing at his full 6'3" crumbled. Overnight, it seemed, Stanley was stooped, and his blue eyes had the clouded look of a very old man. For Stanley a day care center could have been adrenalin in his life's blood. Unfortunately, no such center existed where he lived.

Would you expect Herman Miller to go to such a center? All his life up early, and out to the factory. He looks down at his big hands which once could lift the most lumber in the loading yard. The calluses are soft now like the rest of him. These big fingers will never shuffle dominoes, but still, the days are long and the nights longer since he's alone. Herman might try the center—just once.

And of course there's Nettie Palmer, widowed only last year. She and Milton always did live quietly, and somehow they were enough for each other. No children, not many friends, just the two of them reading together, eating to-gether, watching TV together. And now here she is, all alone, and probably no one even knows or cares to know. Nettie isn't old-old, but she's getting sick from not eating, and she's wondering more every day why she didn't save up those sleeping pills and just be done with empty days. Nettie, discovered, might be a perfect day care candidate.

There is angry Ferris Jackson, who loves a big political argument, and there's Rosie Jackson, who'd like to get away from his noisy battling. What about Bess Lindley, halted by a stroke, almost non-speaking now, but needful of people and current events and book reviews and reminders that while the mind can function, the crippled body cannot hold one back?

Then old Felicia Robbins, almost blind with cataracts, can hardly find her way around her bedroom in her daughter's home. And Betty, the daughter, half sick with frustration and guilt and fatigue, is ready to put Felicia in any nursing facility —that is, until she hears that there is a day care center where Felicia can go everyday and sometimes on weekends if Betty and her family want to leave town.

Many (or most) of the people who come to day centers are living out the self-fulfilling prophecy that they are hopeless and can, indeed, accomplish nothing. Many are impaired and have limited potential. Others are "functionally impaired," living at a state far below their capacity.

For example, Mavis Williams, once a top legal secretary, was brought to the day care center by her niece with whom she lived. The niece reported that Mavis would not dress unless urged and helped. She never cleaned herself or brushed her hair. Her whole day was spent in passivity, and the family was ready to institutionalize Mavis—and as soon as possible.

The same passivity Mavis had exhibited at home was evident at the day care center. She took the same chair every morning and spent her day looking out the window, ignoring everyone around her. Shortly before Christmas the center director pulled up a chair by Mavis and, without preliminary, said, "Miss Williams, I wonder if I could call on you for some help."

Mavis stirred in her chair. The director continued, "What

with Christmas coming up, I am so far behind I can't seem to catch up on anything. We're planning a bus trip for all the center folks, but I need a list of everyone to check the roll." She paused, then said with some urgency, "Do you suppose —just this once—could you help me by typing up the list and typing name tags for all the people who will be taking the trip?"

Mavis did not answer for a long time, though it seemed as if she sat up a bit straighter. Finally she faced the director and said slowly, "I'll make a lot of mistakes."

"Doesn't matter. We have bottles of liquid paper to blot out the errors."

Mavis typed the lists. Within a couple of months she was a volunteer at the center, responsible for correspondence, menu making, and some reports. Mavis's life has changed. So has that of her niece and family.

Professional persons, leaders in the rehabilitative care of "frail elderly" people, have recognized the need for interval facilities or intermediate kinds of care required by many older people existing on a border between independence and total dependence.

Many authorities have advocated a spectrum of services for the aged, ranging from seven-day-a-week programs in order that family members can have vacations to short-term but intensive outpatient programs for persons with immediate and intensive health needs.

Some day care centers are designed for ambulatory patients so that socialization can take place and/or family members can hold down jobs. Others are designed to be part of 24-hour-a-day institutions. Still another possibility is the geriatric assessment clinic where older people can go for medical evaluation perhaps prior to making a decision about placement.

Premature institutionalization is costly. That fact can be documented by a report of the Department of Health, Education, and Welfare which states that an estimated 250,000 to 500,000 persons become full-time residents in institutions each year for reasons other than medical needs. The report adds that from 1963 to 1969 the number of persons over 65 in nursing and personal care homes increased 47 percent while the aged population increased only 9 percent.

Sometimes the day care facility can help a person who is waiting to be admitted to an institution. Or it can delay institutionalization for some period of time. Also, the center can simply provide needed socialization and support for a person able to exist in the community but doing so at great emotional stress because of loneliness and alienation. Thus, while people may attend the center for varying reasons, they can all find within its program helpful elements to maintain their individuality and "personhood."

An analogy may well be made between the treatment given to some mentally ill persons and that rendered to some impaired older people. A young woman who suffered from a long-term and serious mental illness was able, when she grew better, to discuss some of her "sick" feelings. She talked of her months of being in a catatonic state, unmoving, non-speaking, and seemingly unknowing.

"Did you know what was going on?" she was asked.

"I was aware of many happenings, even though time telescoped and was often out of focus for me."

She was asked whether or not she was aware of people and of events. She responded that one physician, acting in official capacity, came into her room. He was followed by a group of students who watched him lift her eyelids, raise her arm and let it fall, pinch her flesh. Then, without a a glance at her, the physician said, "That is a classic picture of catatonia."

The patient heard the words. She was a "thing." A classic symptom.

"But were there others?" she was asked. Did anyone regard you as other than a non-functioning being?"

She replied that there had been one physician who came in to see her every day, who forced baby food through her unyielding lips, who spoke to her of many things, who regarded her tenderly and gently even though she gave no sign for weeks and months that she could hear or absorb any of his words.

"And you know," she said, "when I finally could manage

to talk, it was to this man who had regarded my humanness through all of the weeks."

Many of the people who come to the day care centers are those who have felt shunted aside by a young society and who now seem wholly unresponsive to others. In the center they should be able to find those persons who will respond to the "areas of wellness" which exist within them.

The Beginnings

Is day care, then, the answer to the problems of the "frail elderly" and the chronically ill? Will the resident population of nursing homes diminish as persons are maintained in their own homes or in the homes of relatives at night, availing themselves of day care facilities during waking hours? Will the costs of care for persons with needs for supportive services plummet as such day programs are developed?

The answers are as complex as the questions raised. Everyone would like to find simple answers. However, studies have shown that day care centers are beneficial (in certain instances); practical (for some people); and less costly than nursing homes (on some bases).

Perhaps it would be helpful first to define what is meant by "therapeutic day care" and then to examine some of the patterns which have been developed.

The surge of interest began when Congress passed an act (P.L. 92–603, Section 222 [Social Security Amendments of 1972]) authorizing "an experimental program to provide Day Care Services for individuals eligible to enroll in the supplemental medical insurance program established under Part B of Title XVIII and Title XIX of the Social Security Act, in Day Care Centers which meet such standards as the Secretary shall by regulation establish."

This action gave hope that Medicare and Medicaid funds might be used for day care. Thus, as a rush to establish centers ensued, it became apparent that a definition of day care must be formulated. Was the term to encompass recreational and continuing education programs for older persons? Or

was it to mean a socialization (and minimum health maintenance and nutrition) effort for isolated or slightly impaired
persons? Or, indeed, was it to be a day hospital requiring
registered nurses and a team of health care personnel? Some
day care facilities act as post-hospital service areas for persons needing restorative aids; others may give a great deal of
psychosocial service to those people needing such care.

In June 1974 six contracts were awarded for experimental
programs. The two programs receiving the combined day
care and homemaker service approach were the San Francisco Home Health Service and the Lexington–Fayette
County Health Department. Contracts for day care services
only were awarded to Burke Rehabilitation Center in White
Plains, New York, and to St. Camillus Nursing Home in Syra-
cuse, New York. Two other contracts—for homemaker services only—were given to Inter-City Home Health Association in Los Angeles and Homemaker–Home Health Aide
Services of Rhode Island. A seventh award was made to
Medicus, Inc., to evaluate the effectiveness of the experimental program.

Staff from the Bureau of Health Services Research worked
with the staff from the Bureau of Health Insurance of the
Social Security Administration and under the umbrella of an
Interagency Task Force (Department of Health, Education,
and Welfare) to try to plan research design and methodology.

For the convenience of the initial working groups, the
following definition of "day care" was developed:

Day Care is a program of services provided under health leadership
in an ambulatory care setting for adults who do not require 24-hour
institutional care and yet, due to physical and/or mental impairment, are not capable of full-time independent living. Participants
in the day care program are referred to the program by their attending physician or by some other appropriate source such as an
institutional discharge planning program, a welfare agency, etc.
The essential elements of a day-care program are directly toward
meeting the health maintenance and restoration needs of participants. However, there are socialization elements in the program
which, by overcoming the isolation so often associated with illness
in the aged and disabled, are considered vital for the purposes of

fostering and maintaining the maximum possible state of health and well-being.[1]

One of the new directions of current day care programs is that, instead of being set up for persons with mental problems, they are planned for persons who might otherwise need institutionalization because of chronic illness or disability.

In order to predict what day care might become, it was necessary to learn what already exists, what was effective or ineffective and why, what programs cost, and other facts about them. TransCentury Corporation of Washington was given a contract to examine systematically representative programs now operating.

The findings reveal:

1 Two models emerged, differentiated largely by the services provided, staffing patterns, and participant characteristics.
2 Model I is characterized by its relatively heavy emphasis on health services. It has a high ratio of registered nurses and professional, including physical, occupational, and speech therapists.
3 Most Model I participants have recently suffered serious illness and need rehabilitative care. An average of 48 percent are paralyzed to some degree. Many use wheelchairs, and most are dependent in three or more activities of daily living.
4 Model II emphasizes daytime supervision for generally less-impaired participants. Staffing patterns show a smaller proportion of professional nurses and few therapists with more nursing and therapy services provided by aides than in Model I.
5 Model II participants for the most part suffer the infirmities of old age and are less apt to be in a rehabilitative stage of chronic illness. An average of 16 percent are paralyzed to some degree, but most are dependent in fewer than two activities of daily living, and many are independent.
6 A tendency, on average, to give appropriate care is a special strength of adult day care programs. The 10 programs studied have developed an amazingly close match between staff health care capability and the needs of participants. Programs with the most impaired and dependent participants have the highest ratios of health care professionals, and they put the

most emphasis on health care services, especially emphasiz-
ing therapies . . .

7 However, in some programs, a small number of participants
—too small to show up statistically—need more therapy than
they can get from the program. These participants are the
exception, however.

8 The close match between staff skills and participants also
confirms that a few programs have neither participants with
many health care needs, nor staff with particularly strong
health care capabilities. Should these be considered adult day
care?

9 What constitutes a therapy, especially occupational therapy,
needs to be better defined by Model II programs.

10 The average per diem cost for the nine most typically costly
programs is $21. One program is exceptionally expensive, at
$61.56. It is one of the two rehabilitative programs of Model
I. However, the other similar program costs only $24.51.[2]

The Costs

Day care programs nationally have not proved to be substantially less costly than nursing home care. In some instances,
the cost may be more. In the TransCentury studies of ten
centers, the two models of day care varied greatly in cost.
Taking the average cost of care in a nursing home at about
$18 per day, the general per diem cost for 9 of the 19 day
care centers, at $21.04, does not make such facilities desir-
able simply on the basis of cost effectiveness. However, the
researchers have stated that they believe that day care costs
may be slightly overestimated (because they include in-kind
contributions and volunteer help), while the nursing home
costs may be underrated because those contributions are not
included. The research team estimates that nursing home
costs might go up by $2 to $5 per day on that basis.[3]

Another reason stated for the apparently higher cost of day
care is that many of the day care centers are still in the
developing stages and will be able, in the future, to encompass a larger population without substantially raising the cost
of care.

Comparisons are difficult to obtain, again, because there

are no data which show the total cost of maintaining an elderly person in some setting other than a nursing home. For example, the additional costs incurred for the day care resident include housing, food, transportation, and other incidentals. The dilemma might be seen thus:

The average day care resident might attend only 10 to 12 days a month. The program then might reflect $210 per client—ten days at $21 a day. The resident of the nursing home uses those facilities 30 days a month at perhaps $20 per day and the total cost is $600. If, however, the "extra costs" incurred by the non-nursing home resident come to as much as $390 a month, the nursing home route might be more cost effective.

The cost factor in day care remains one of the chief difficulties in planning expansion. The TransCentury Corporation stated that state Medicaid officials might hesitate to establish a per diem rate for the program when not all services are health-related. Despite the fact that health services are part of the "package," the officials often feel reluctant to pick up the total amount.

A solution, according to the TransCentury report, would be to set reimbursement figures on a combined fee-for-service and inclusive rate basis. They state the possibilities as follows:

. . . Such components as meals, transportation, recreation, social services, patient supervision, and assistance and nursing are included in any core program. Reimbursement could be set at the base rate equal to the costs of providing those core services. Any additional service, e.g., physical therapy, psychological counseling, speech therapy, and so on, would be reimbursed on a fee-for-service basis, i.e., only when such services were actually received. Quality of core standards would be enforced through this mechanism, if desired, by requiring certain minimum licensing/certification standards for staff providing these services and specified treatment modalities in order to qualify for reimbursement.[4]

Such separation of costs and reimbursement could probably prove to be cost effective. For the "adequate" older person who needs primarily social and nutritional supports, the basic day care plan would provide needed services. The greatest cost benefits might come in terms of the "frail elderly," those persons who need a broad support system in order to stay in the community. For them, if Medicaid could reimburse for care outside the institution, the more desirable and overall lower cost plan of day care plus the needed health services could delay or postpone for an indefinite period the time of going to an institution for total 24-hour-a-day care.

In any such system as this, a functional cost-accounting system would have to be developed. The cost effectiveness of day care as compared with nursing home care has been subject to discussion and disagreement. Most concerned people agree that the humanitarian aspects of day care for those people who want to maintain themselves in a community setting make the cost effectiveness a secondary rather than primary consideration. However, some studies do underscore the financial feasibility of day care.

One such study is entitled "Cost-Benefit Analysis of Alternative Care Programs for the Elderly." Completed by N. Doherty, B. Hicks, and N. Stilwell of the University of Connecticut Health Center in Farmington, Connecticut, their analysis showed a potential savings in providing day care for certain client groups. However, they stated that it is important to consider the total life-support costs, including home meals, medicines, and other items, in order to obtain a meaningful comparison of the two types of care.

Another study, "Cost-Effectiveness of Geriatric Day Care" by H. Lohn, E. R. McCuan, and J. Hsu of the Levindale Geriatric Research Center in Baltimore, Maryland, reported that geriatric day care is a cost-effective alternative to long-term care for the chronically ill and impaired aged. The three-year longitudinal study of day care and inpatient care showed that persons in the day care center were kept at comparable or improved functional levels over a period of time, while a matched sample of inpatients showed decline over the same period. And the costs in day care were less than those in the institution.

Nursing homes and 24-hour-a-day institutional care facilities are important and needed—but for those who should appropriately be placed there. In the health care field for all ages, there is increasing awareness of the feasibility of day hospitals and night hospitals, for convalescent facilities, and for home health aides in order to cut down lengthy hospitalization in an expensive facility.

Final accounting shows that nursing home care is more economical if a person attends day care more than 15 days a month. The most cost-effective program, according to the researchers, is one which serves a large number of people, each for only a few days a month.[5] The researchers are careful to explain that their statements apply to those persons who would need institutional care if there were no day care alternative. Finally, they feel that for the majority of participants in Model I programs and about half of those in Model II, the day care approach is indeed cost effective. An additional population might be reached by bringing out of nursing homes the estimated 40 percent who might not need to be there if alternative facilities were available. In some instances, payment to families to help with care of the older person could help to maintain home vs. institutional care.

Day care centers might prove cost effective if they enable one other family member to work outside the home and thus increase family income. Cost effectiveness cannot, of course, measure the mental health aspects of the day care program versus the nursing home. For many people the socialization and independence fostered through day care make it a worthwhile and exciting alternative.

The loneliness, isolation, and needs of older people cannot be charted on a financial graph. For many, the day care center offers a workable method for continuing to live as human beings, welcome in their communities. The "extended family" concept offered by the centers helps prolong life with meaning for many aging persons.

Day care centers infuse the extended family concept into lives of many older people. They add a dimension of participation often lacking. As Dr. Robert Havighurst puts it:

The majority of aging and aged adults in the United States do not live in institutions. Rather, they remain in their communities and manage without the help of organized social services. When families and individuals require social intervention because of age-related needs, the capability of communities to respond effectively and efficiently is often deficient. Flexible and alternative programs for providing income maintenance, health services, housing, and work and leisure activities are often either not apparent to the persons in need or are not, in fact available.[6]

Piecemeal funding has made the organization of day care centers difficult. An example of this fragmented funding can be seen in the following statement:

Three titles of the Older Americans Act (III, IV, VII) have provided funds for some services in some centers through Federal, State, and local levels of government; three titles (VI and XVI and more recently XX) of the Social Security Act; Model Cities and revenue sharing moneys have been tapped; Medicare and Medicaid have paid for eligible services; a variety of community organizations— United Way, in some instances private insurors—have paid for services; and in-kind and volunteer services have been utilized. Participant fees make up a relatively small proportion of revenues.[7]

Day Care Analyzed

The growing concern about day care centers as options for older people who cannot function well alone has been evidenced in research and demonstration projects. One study prepared for the Division of Long-Term Care of HEW has been concerned with finding what presently exists in the day care field and what elements of programs seem to lead to success.

The researchers discovered that although day care is a service which may provide alternatives to institutionalization, the concept itself is ambiguous and often confusing. Wide variations exist in the size of centers, staffing patterns, in criteria, programs, and other elements.[8]

Some of the major points they discovered in an analysis of 15 centers were as follows:

1. The average size of a day care center is 40 people. However, these figures do not reveal the capacity of each center because the proportion of full-time and part-time participants is not broken down.

2. The demographic characteristics showed that minority representation was 49 percent of the group (based in great part upon the location of the centers). More than half live alone; about one fourth with a spouse. Eighty percent of the participants have an income of $2,000 a year or less. The age range for almost half was 69 years or younger.

3. Admission criteria varied greatly. Most included the client's ability to be ambulatory, to be able to pay for some portion of the services, and to be considered unharmful. Findings also included the fact that most who left the day care center returned to the community or entered some kind of institution but were not off the rolls because of death.

4. No consistent association existed between the length of stay and the perceived service objective.

5. Since cost information was not given by all the centers, a comparative cost estimate could not be made.

6. Staffing patterns were diverse. Full-time professionals ranged from 15 to one, and staff-to-participant ratio ranged from one to one to one to 32.

7. Services to meet physical care needs varied widely. Professional nursing services were available in 14 centers, but the time the nurse spent ranged from substantial to negligible. The same held true for professional social work. All centers reported therapeutic recreational activities.

The researchers concluded that "Day care centers are one alternative form of service delivery designed to meet the needs of chronically ill and disabled aged persons. It is a service innovation that appears to have value in reducing the likelihood of unnecessary institutionalization. However, this service concept must be considered as only one step in the continuum of care. It does not replace the need for institutional care for those aged persons who are too impaired to be maintained in the community. Future planning activities must be based on a full understanding of the benefits and limitations of day care services, and rational social policies must be developed to insure appropriate expansion of alternatives to institutional care."[9]

Five goals were set by Hawaii, which in 1972 became the first state to enact legislation on day care for the elderly. The goals were:

- To keep welfare-related individuals out of institutions as long as possible.
- To provide social contact and enrichment experiences.
- To make burdens lighter for the younger family and adult children who work.
- To provide a nutritional program and pleasant surroundings for those of the elderly who would be very much alone.
- To provide transportation in some form . . . for travel to clinics, dentists, and doctors' offices, therapists, recreational trips, adult education classes, as well as normal travel to and from the center.[10]

These basic goals have pretty much been followed by many other groups setting up day care centers. However, the primary goal is still to restore meaning and function to old people who, because of conditions of health, finances, or location, have been removed from the central areas of experience.

Because the needs of the "frail elderly" may change for better or worse, it becomes imperative that all types of services be available on a changeover basis as clients require either more intensive or less intensive services.

The current goal for the "frail elderly" seems to be less an "either–or" and more an ongoing plan of services—a continuum of options for living patterns.

Herbert Shore, Executive Director of the Dallas Home and Hospital for Jewish Aged, has set out the following eight objectives of day care:

1 To give an older person an opportunity to take part in a variety of activities during the day and early evening.
2 To provide a semi-protective environment.
3 When appropriate, to delay or to reduce the need for permanent placement in the home.
4 To provide a balanced diet.
5 To use the day care program as a testing experience for the applicant to the home, when there are questions as to kind of care needed or the ability of the applicant to adjust.
6 As part of a treatment plan to relieve tensions in family situations.
7 To meet needs for those waiting to enter if space is not available.

8 To maximize use of facilities without needing to expand or build.[11]

Since the day care program does not include intensive health services except in emergencies, the client should come with information about his personal physician. A physical examination and results should be given to the staff prior to the client's admittance, and should include information regarding limitation on activities, special diet, medication (kind, dosage, and whether or not the individual is capable of taking it himself), and other considerations which have to do with the client's health.

Some written agreement concerning medical emergency care should be formulated, and the staff should be conversant with first aid techniques. Whether or not the center is set up as a hospital adjunctive facility, it still attracts those "frail elderly" who have health and impairment problems which may pose emergencies.

Also, a dietician will need to be a consultant if not the planner of meals in the center. Many clients have suffered from effects of malnutrition. Where meals come in from an institution, the dietician can do all the planning. If kitchens are available at the center, clients can assist with meal planning and even with preparation. At any rate, a morning and mid-afternoon snack should be available as well as a hot noon meal.

Night Care and "Sitters"

In addition to day care centers, it has been proposed that night care centers should be instituted. Day care centers permit families to work while placing their parents in a safe and comfortable environment. Night care centers could help keep the core family intact by permitting children to go out for the evening without fear for the safety of the aging parent and without guilt and worry.

"Sitters" might offer still another service on behalf of older persons who cannot be left alone. A core of persons trained to be watchful and helpful with older people could perform important functions in many households.

Looking at the greatly varied needs of older people, it becomes clear that some kind of classification of older people should be made. Dr. Eric Pfeiffer has proposed that we first divide the elderly in the United States into those who are very well and need nothing more than the usual attention needed by people of any age and the disabled who require some kind of service. Since this classification is too broad, Dr. Pfeiffer suggests a more useful scheme would be a multidimensional system for assessing the functional level of persons in each of these five categories:

1 physical functioning
2 psychological functioning
3 social resources
4 economic resources
5 activities of daily living

Using this system, persons could then be further rated on each dimension, according to these functional levels:

1 outstanding function
2 average function
3 mild impairment
4 moderate impairment
5 severe impairment
6 total impairment[12]

Day Care Services

Some of the services provided in comprehensive day care centers include a number of self-care as well as leisure activities. Self-care activities include grooming, such as proper dress and cleanliness. The addition of barber and beauty shop aids will often spur older people into renewed pride in personal appearance. Group mending and laundromat services will also help older people keep their clothes presentable.

In order to increase personal competence home safety should be taught, with much attention to accident prevention. Lip-reading is a helpful technique for those who are losing their hearing.

Reality orientation helps the clients keep themselves oriented in time and place in a world which too often, for them, seems to be shifting and changing. Days, events, names, and competences too often for the confused older person may seem to be multicolored balloons whose strings slip from aging fingers.

Occupational and physical therapy are two important phases of good day care programs. Many of the infirmities of old age come as much from disuse as from disability. Many recreational programs also help with the limbering of fingers, feet, and backs. Mending, crocheting, building, walking—all aid in keeping bodies limber and functional.

Within the category of leisure-time activities are included physical exercises, financially productive sheltered workshops, and educational programs of interest to the clients. Activities encouraging creativity and group functions such as trips are vital to the success of such a program. And, of course, activities on behalf of others are vital.

Day care centers differ from other types of facilities for older people in that while they are set up primarily for socialization, they encourage the "frail elderly" or those with moderate handicaps to participate. Persons may come into day care because they are lonely and need contact with other people or because they have a health condition requiring supervision and aid.

In good day care a combination of services is offered—nutrition, health, social, and recreational. Although sophisticated health services are not provided, staff members would have first-aid training and should have physicians' instructions about care for persons in the program.

The day care center differs from the senior center in its supervisory and health aspects. Senior centers are primarily social settings for able older persons who want to get together for pleasant daytime activities and mutual sharing of good experiences.

The day hospital, on the other hand, is primarily health related, admitting those persons who need help after hospitalization or who may be kept from hospitalization through daytime care. The day hospital staff includes skilled nurses, in addition to physical and occupational therapy and social work services. Socializing is part of such a program also.

Ideally, these varied community programs will be "swinging door" services in that a person may go from one to the other, and not necessarily from less intensive to more intensive supervision. Some older persons may need a day hospital setting for a period and may improve so much that they can function with the aid of a day care center. Without having to battle the idea of irreversible conditions, they may be able, like their younger counterparts, to find flexible patterns of maintaining themselves within their communities.

Several considerations underlie the obvious concerns about people growing old—lack of money, too little medical care, needs for good nutrition. However, the population "carrying" the old in our society may too often look upon the leisure that the older generation has as a bonus rather than a burden. Because the young, the middle-aged, and the young old too frequently are harassed by stressful jobs and rushed days, they may not stop to consider that only the very young and the very old have time. During weeks when a game of tennis or an hour's jogging or a dip in the backyard pool have to be programmed and "worked in," it seems as if leisure would be the most cherished possession in the world.

Yet ironically, because the younger generation does not have or use leisure for the development of crafts and hobbies and sports, they find themselves too often idle and miserable when the work doors have shut and time opens up.

Thus, in planning for alternate kinds of programs for older people, much consideration has to be given to the development of leisure-time activities which can entice the clients to participate. "Fun and games" have been reserved for the young in our society, and adults frequently participate only to please youthful charges and to keep them occupied. Work has been valued and play ignored. As consideration has gone toward provision of care facilities for older people, emphasis has been placed on physical surroundings and nutritional programs. With basic areas of need considered, it becomes apparent that much thought must be given to how to feed the "inner person" who might avail himself of the day care facilities.

Are there ways of infusing meaning into life, like insulin

into the body of a diabetic? Can crafts and hobbies take on meaning other than self-gratification? Many persons working with older people have considered the mutual responsibilities which older and younger people might have for one another. The talents and knowledge and skills of the elder generation have, in many instances, been "swapped" for the abilities of the younger ones.

Recommendations for adult day care have been stated thus

Recommendations for adult day care should involve, first of all, an affirmation of public policy which supports such programs as a means of protecting the health and safety of those persons whose disabilities require the services provided in such centers. Implementation of this policy will involve an investment in furthering the development of such centers and clarifying their functions and purposes in the following ways:

Through a series of demonstrations adequately funded over sufficient time which will test and evaluate the various service combinations and their appropriateness to various population groups in different geographic community settings.

Through an organized approach to the development of administrative methods, program size, program organization, and program policies utilizing the expertise of those who are presently involved in delivering such services.

Through research approaches focused upon utilization patterns, longitudinal studies, and projected costs in various service combinations.

Through the provision of organized training opportunities in adult day care for members of the medical profession and other health professionals as well as paraprofessionals.

Through the development of a rational funding pattern which will eliminate current fragmentation of funding sources and an initial approach to guidelines which may be developed as mandates to states and communities.

Through the development of materials which will assist communities in the organization of such centers and interpret their function to the professions and to the public at large.[13]

An important difference between the day care center and senior center is the motivation of persons in the program.

Perhaps one of the greatest benefits of the day care facility comes in service to the lonely and isolated older person who will not, on his own, seek out help. Many suffer from depression and have fallen into a pattern of defeat and misery. The inertia they feel may keep them functioning at far less than their capacity. Those around them soon cease expecting any independent activity from them, and, in the nature of a self-fulfilling prophecy, the activities of the person deteriorate.

Here the day care center can be a psychological "upper." Staff attitudes and program can express to the client that he is able to function at a level higher. Ongoing interaction and an attitude of realistic hopefulness will have a positive effect on the majority of clients.

Anyone who has had contact with mentally ill persons and has seen their ability to mobilize themselves in certain positive atmospheres knows the residual abilities most people have to rise to occasions. In the day care center an older person has the opportunity to test himself against others, to be set into the center of reality if he is confused, to socialize, and to move outside his own perimeters.

Good day care centers also involve the clients in selecting their own activities and foods. Staff will call upon the participants to do all they are capable of or willing to do in terms of self-care or help in the center itself. Women (or men) skilled at cooking may like to plan or to prepare foods occasionally. Clients may help in many ways, such as setting tables or making curtains.

Involving older persons in the welfare of others is an important ingredient in any good day care center. Many older persons have grown inward, have almost forgotten how to feel responsible for others or to reach out to them. It is important for center staff to encourage older people to "do for" others. For example, if young people come to give shampoos, visit, sing, play games, or take older persons on shopping expeditions, center clients should be enticed to make cookies and have a party for their young sponsors or to knit belts or caps for the young people or in some other manner demonstrate the reciprocal nature of the relationship.

An example of how this works can be seen in results from

a study on remotivation of chronically ill geriatric patients. Thirty-six patients were paired with 36 elementary school students and 36 control patients. Using specific remotivation techniques, the experimental patients and students met biweekly for three and a half months. The experimental subjects improved much more in several areas than the control group.

On the personal side, ward personnel observed that the patients anticipated students' visits by requesting showers and clean clothing and frequently getting small treats for the young people. They welcomed the students and laughed and talked with them and participated in scheduled activities.[14]

Mixing generations often proves beneficial for both age groups. However, one of the most important aspects of the interaction is to keep older persons motivated toward thinking and doing for others instead of accepting services without a sense of responsibility for demonstrating their appreciation.

For the old person feeling impotent and useless, a day care center surrounding can restore a sense of control of his or her own destiny and a sense of worth. Even the pleasure of participating in decision-making may return some of the feeling of independence and value.

Auxiliary Benefits

Certain auxiliary functions can be performed in day care centers simply because older persons in the centers may need various aids and be unaware of community resources for obtaining them. One important role is that of advocate for the older person, who may have little sophistication about dealing with the "system," or may be intimidated by institutional processes.

For example, Andy Hernandez, with his six years in the army, a dozen years of work on the railroad, and almost three decades as a street cleaner, failed to receive his Veterans Administration check for three months. One day he summoned the courage to ask timidly the center director what she thought might have gone wrong. He needed the money, but he was afraid to ask. Also, his recovery from serious surgery had left him weak and extremely low in energy.

The entire staff took up the cause of Andy Hernandez. They worked for four weeks, making visits to the Veterans Administration office, talking with Mr. Hernandez, telephoning the post office, visiting the Regional Veterans Administration office, and following every lead possible. At the end of that time, Mr. Hernandez received his three past-due checks plus his regular payments every month.

In order to do the best job possible as advocates, center staff should include persons needing help in all the negotiations so they can learn how to obtain aid on their own behalf. This teaching process can well guide the older person toward increased confidence and competence in managing his own affairs.

The center can be a focal point for all kinds of activities on behalf of older people. It may keep records on other available services and help clients find what is most appropriate for them. In this way the center can provide special services without adding still one more office or bureau to be staffed and housed.

Location

Where should day care centers be located? In the center of town near bus stops? In rural areas where there are grounds for picnics and gardens? In various sections of the city? Perhaps the answer to all the questions is affirmative. Centers may function efficiently in a central location or outside of town (if there is transportation). Churches serve as splendid focal points for centers.

Or would neighborhood day care centers, like neighborhood schools, be an improvement over current models? The advantages might be that people who know each other, at least by sight, could attend the same center. A neighborhood location would ease transportation problems. It might also pull together a homogeneous group who share many of the same interests. Some of the day care program could "carry over" into evening and weekend hours when lonely or ill people might be able to call on one another for companionship or help.

The disadvantage, of course, would be that a proliferation of centers might make too many geographical demands on both attending and supervisory staff. Finding and setting up numerous locations might prove a strain on the planners. Still, if the neighborhood concept proved the most workable, it might well be possible to set up supervisory activities in a central location, where staff recruitment and training could go on and nutritious meals, under dietary supervision, could be prepared and delivered to various centers throughout the city. If the centers were small, many kinds of locations might be found for them, some even in neighborhood schools with available space. If the latter were possible, clients might share meals with children, thus accomplishing the dual purpose of having nutritious meals on site and a mix of generations in a natural setting.

Staff Training

Professional and continuing training of day care center staff is a vital aspect of providing a positive climate for center clients. The staff should know how people may demonstrate their feelings of being old, useless, and nonfunctional. They should also be aware that those who go into old age rebelliously, battling against diminution of function and lessening of skills, may be masking their fright about old age. They need to see that depression often covers deep anger, that paranoia may be displacement of inner feelings onto others. Books about schizophrenics who become many different people have fascinated readers and movie-goers. However, in more subtle fashion all of us are many different people and all of us wear many masks.

The seemingly agreeable little woman who nods at every suggestion in a day care center may be hiding an enormous load of hostility and anger. The boastful man may be covering a great deal of insecurity. Older people who have been isolated for months or years and who have grown to think principally in terms of themselves and their body functions may need many kinds of enticements to move into a broader roadway of living. It is not enough that center staff be pleasant and interested. They must also have the training to recognize some of the hidden messages given by the old people.

Although the center is not set up to be a miniature psychiatric unit, all staff can be alert to possible need for psychiatric help. Many problems evidenced by older people can be alleviated immediately by early recognition and assistance by caring people alert to signs of mental disability. Intervention at initial stages can often be far speedier and more effective than ameliorative programs at later stages.

Every person who comes in contact with the day care client should be aware of the effect his own attitude will have on the person with whom he is dealing.

The staff should be trained in simple first aid. There should be a dietician or dietary supervision for the one hot meal served during the day. All the people who work in the center should certainly be trained to be supportive, positive in outlook, and helpful.

In the day hospital, health is obviously the major consideration. Most of the clients are returning from a 24-hour-a day hospitalization or are awaiting entrance into such a facility. Many require rehabilitation, as from the effects of a stroke. Sometimes persons who are quite confused are permitted to attend the day hospital program.

The psychiatric day hospital centers primarily on the confused person and the mentally ill. The tie-in between the psychiatric day hospital and a regular hospital facility is very close. Patients stay in a psychiatric day hospital for a shorter period than is possible in a day care center. They may move in either direction—toward a 24-hour-a-day facility or into the day care center.

While the definitions of the various facilities seem clearcut, their operation is less so. Some day care centers have health programs of lesser or greater degree. Some day hospitals have socialization programs of some significance.

Of course, no one program is a panacea. Day care programs are no exception. For some people they may be prayers answered, with built-in friends, care, and recreation. For others they may offer little and be a chore instead of a bonus. The offerings of a day care center might fit totally into the lifestyle of certain older people. For others, they may be too simplistic or nonstimulating.

Day care centers do not exist in a vacuum. Clients come from somewhere and return to some place—most often to the home of a son or daughter. Families have much to do with the success or failure of the day care center program, and the center has much to do with the success of the older person in the family home. Therefore, enlisting the family in discussions of the clients' welfare is an important part of good day care treatment. If the program consists of a good deal of reality orientation and consistent behavior toward independence, that same type of activity should be carried on when the client returns home. If certain techniques have been found effective in working with the older person, those techniques should be mutually examined. Resources such as community mental health centers should be identified and contacted in case of difficulty.

The family should be able also to share, without guilt, some of the feelings which surface in caring for the old person and some of the needs family members have for privacy or relief. Pooling information about "after hours" care can help both parties learn more effective coping mechanisms.

In the case where the center client is living with a spouse, the spouse should be enlisted in the overall care program and in planning activities after hours.

And what about the client himself? Is everything to be planned "for" and not "with"? No indeed.

All persons should be invited individually or collectively to be a part of the decision-making process in regard to activities, behavior, ongoing programs, and future plans. A council of clients can speak for the group, but each person should be a part of program planning and the process of decision making. Staff can serve to suggest, but clients should be the primary planners of their own welfare.

Integrating Day Care and Institution

Integrating a day care program into an already existing facility can prove to be cost effective and serve as a life-enhancing program both to the residents of the 24-hour-a-day facility and to persons involved in day care. However, there are some negative aspects to such a plan.

Residents may regard the day participants as intruders and may resist their participating in activities. The same can hold true for staff, who may feel that their efforts toward the permanent clients are diluted by the new and temporary group.

In one instance where such jealousies and difficulties arose, the social worker and nurse coordinator tried to solve the problem by having group meetings of day care participants. The meetings were geared toward having the participants join in planning their recreational activities. Group decisions were made also for other aspects of the program, such as food services or transportation. Interestingly, although the group was willing to discuss activities and possibilities, they would not talk about personal affairs or problems and even resented the fact that one person attempted to bring personal matters into the group sessions.

On the other hand, the social worker found that families of clients were more open about discussing interpersonal relationships. Children seemed willing to talk about feelings and actions concerning parents and to plan for ways in which the program itself could be improved.[15]

The cost factor also needs to be managed. Depending on whether the client attends every day, all day, or on an occasional basis, and depending on whether or not the program is subsidized by community or other funds, costs may vary as greatly as less than $1 per person to many dollars per day.

In order to counteract the resistance of institution staff, much pre-planning needs to be done. First of all, staff members have to be assured that their own duties will not be increased but that auxiliary staff will take care of extra loads. Everyone involved with the day care clients should also be in on the planning with the staff so that there will be clarification of duties and responsibilities.

Pleasant, adequate facilities need to be available for the day care client without detracting from those for the residents. These arrangements should include comfortable lounge chairs, a working television set, game tables, and places for crafts and for reading.

Careful interpretation to the resident group should be made. This step is as important as the work with the staff. When such insightful planning takes place, the day care program has a greater chance for continuing success.

Day Hospitals

Day hospitals provide a special service for disabled older people. On the one hand, they can shorten hospitalization for a person suffering from a long-term disability such as stroke or arthritis. On the other, they can provide rehabilitative services which improve a patient's physical and mental health. Still another service is that offered to patients' families. With the advent of day hospitals, family members can often bring the older person home for brief periods rather than submit him or her to long-time hospitalization or institutionalization.

For the patient himself, the day hospital can mean renewed hope of self-sufficiency. Perhaps Margo Phillips can tell it best.

Margo, lively, lovely, and hard-working, had scarcely slowed her pace in the years from 40 to 50 and now to 65. A ladies' wear buyer, she had kept herself svelte and groomed in a fashion befitting her profession. She worked nights and weekends. She traveled. She read. And she neglected physical checkups. Although she had felt some dizziness and had suffered headaches for several years, she had not taken the time for a thorough physical.

The stroke caught her unsuspecting and unprepared. It was at midnight just as she had finished closing her suitcase for the morning flight to New York. And it was ten the next morning, when someone called her office to say that she was found on the floor of her apartment, semi-conscious.

Margo's natural stamina and determination helped her through the first phase of the stroke. It was then that depression hit, a bomb which shattered her life meaning and left her being scattered on the battlefield of her illness.

She did not want to live. She did not want to be a slobbering, unkempt woman. She refused to turn into a clumsy basketmaker. She wanted to die. But life would not let go of Margo, and after painful weeks she faced the fact that she would have to endure and begin slow rehabilitation.

Restorative powers took over. Margo, accustomed to making decisions, began to plan her future. First she had a hairdresser come into her hospital room and style her hair in a fashion she could manage with one hand. Then she learned to put on makeup with her left hand. And then she talked with the social worker at the hospital.

Fortunately, the hospital was associated with a day hospital, and Margo planned to use it. She found a woman to spend the nights with her in her apartment and went to the day hospital for rehabilitative exercises, including physical and speech therapy and psychological consultation.

Without the day hospital Margo might have remained for some months in the hospital or a nursing home, initiative diminished, her sense of competence all but erased, and her decision-making powers decreased. Total hospitalization could easily have added to Margo's already-formed depression and crushed the resurgence of will she began to experience.

As it was, Margo asked that fashion magazines and paperwork be brought to her at her apartment, and in a matter of weeks she was carrying out many of her tasks in the fashion market. For her the day hospital provided needed help toward independence.

It was different with Jake Mason. He too had been active all his life, but physically. As a boy, he had spent summers in a logging camp. As a man he had served in almost every capacity on a construction crew. Winter days and wet ones, tired or well, Jake had been at work. Nothing could down him. Or so he thought.

The arthritis was slow at first—a sore wrist or fingers that wouldn't handle right. And then it was his feet and joints in his legs. Before long Jake could not pretend. He could not work. He would be a cripple. Like Margo, Jake underwent depression and despair. If he could not work, life was not worth living.

And there was Jake in the little house with Margaret frantic and the money dwindling. She took her two weeks' vacation from her job at the school cafeteria and looked for some way to care for Jake and still bring in some money. More than the paycheck, she needed some relief from Jake's complaints and depression and ugly outbursts of anger. She couldn't stand to be with him 24 hours a day, and she was ashamed of feeling so unhappy with her almost-helpless husband.

The two of them would have been locked together in a death grip of anger and depression had it not been for the day hospital in their community. Jake was picked up mornings and returned evenings, and Margaret went on to her job and still had the psychic and physical energy to look after Jake when both came home.

For Jake the day hospital offered hope. In addition to physical therapy he found men who could share some favorite pastimes, like dominoes. And Jake learned also that there were some things his hands could still make, like bird houses and coffee tables. The sanding and polishing equipment helped him use some of the hand muscles which had seemed almost immobilized.

Lunchtime at the day hospital was as therapeutic as the rehabilitation regime. Here Jake found people to talk to, persons with whom he could share news and hopes and a variety of feelings. Seeing other people struggle to regain competence gave him courage to continue his own efforts.

By the time Margo and Jake no longer needed the physical therapy program of a day hospital, they had regained emough emotional and physical competence that they were able to resume life at a level undreamed of immediately after they were stricken. For Margo, part-time work without travel was the answer. For Jake, a day care center was located, and it was there that he could continue with many of his hobbies and fulfill his need for companionship and sustenance.

Originally the day hospital was considered a means of delaying or postponing hospitalization for people needing supervision in the daytime while their families were away. In 1945 the Malborough Day Hospital in England was established in connection with the psychiatric unit of the parent hospital. The concept was expanded from purely psychiatric care to include geriatric patients who required care primarily for physical disabilities, and in 1952 the Cowley Road Day Hospital was established in Oxford.

The concept succeeded and took hold. By 1970, Great Britain had 119 Geriatric Day Hospitals. Some serve fewer than 10 patients a day; others have 50 or more. Overall, more than half the clients attended only one day a week, and 5 percent four or five times a week.

The Lennard Day Hospital in Bromley demonstrates still another model. Here patients, primarily suffering from strokes, fractures, and Parkinson's disease, come on Monday morning and return home on Friday afternoons. To make this kind of program succeed the family and community must provide supportive therapy over the weekend.

The scope and parameters of the day hospital continue to be defined. Should it be strictly physical rehabilitation, or should socialization be part of its function? The physicians and staff who consider the dilemma are aware that lack of socialization can lead to isolation and depression, and can result in physical deterioration and a need for special services. The dilemma is largely unsolved—various day hospitals operate within limits which may differ widely.

The variety of programs offered at Cowley Road Hospital point to the many areas which need to be addressed in trying to give the impaired elderly help they must have to be at least semi-independent. A Cowley assessment team determines what assistance the patient needs to help him learn and manage skills which will keep him functional at home. The ability to do basic chores often makes the difference in whether or not a patient will be able to maintain himself.

For example, the hospital kitchen becomes a teaching room. Here the older person is taught or retaught basic skills in cooking, serving, and washing dishes. Help with meal planning is also given.

The team assesses the patient's ability to keep himself properly. He is given help with personal hygiene. If he cannot take care of his needs without help, he can bathe and groom himself at the center. And he may have his hairdressing and laundry needs provided there.

Even the patient's crafts and recreational activities are constantly assessed by the team. All of his activities are geared toward helping him learn how to function in spite of his disabilities—to maintain himself with a good mental attitude as well.

Transportation and coordination with medical services, including dealing with the patient's physician, seem to be some of the stickiest problems in establishing a day hospital program. The fact that, to date, the costs of many day hospital services have not been reimbursable to the patient has caused the concept to be slow in developing in the United States. Too often the only options have been for the patient to remain in his own home, taxing family members beyond strength and competence, or going to a full-time nursing home where active rehabilitative processes are minimal.

An example of the physical health care model can be seen in the Burke Day Hospital in White Plains, New York. Designated a "hospital without beds," the facility accepts chronically ill people 14 years of age or over. However, as might be expected, close to three fourths of the persons are from 60 years upward.

Burke is affiliated with medical colleges and hospitals and is accredited by the Joint Commission on Accreditation of Hospitals. While it is open five days a week, most patients attend an average of two or three days per week for about six hours a day.

Services include medical care supplied by a hospital physician assisted by a certified nurse practitioner. The staff works in conjunction with the patient's own physician and uses the consultation services of other medical staff available on call.

Psychiatrists are also on stand-by as consultants. These team members serve patients and also provide in-service training for staff. Other specialists are available as needed.

Occupational therapy is built into the Burke process. An occupational therapist serves as supervisor for both the diversionary and functional processes of therapy. Physical therapy is another component of the hospital services. Volunteers are trained to be important caregivers in speech therapy and in discharge and liaison procedures.

Patients are divided into those requiring intensive and intermediate care. Recognizing ever-changing needs, the Burke staff recommends moving patients from one level of care to another as needs arise. A third level is also under consideration, consisting of a preventative program involving many intervention techniques.[16]

Maintaining a relationship with the community has proved a cornerstone on which to build a program like Burke Day Hospital. Staff time spent with community agencies has often helped in reassuring them that the hospital is simply an adjunct to other available services.

The often neglected and forgotten poorer group of older people in the community have had to be sought out vigorously. Housing authorities and social service departments of local hospitals were primary sources of referral for this population.

Reimbursement for the day hospital comes from many sources. The major portion is from Medicare, including Medicare/Medicaid, Medicare/Private Insurance, and Medicare/Self Pay. Major Medical insurance takes care of about 12 percent, and other funds come from State Aid for Children and from self payment.

Is the day hospital cost effective? That question is probably the most difficult to answer. Some of its services are not available anywhere else and thus cannot be compared to other facilities. One basis on which to judge cost effectiveness might be found in the following: Some day hospital patients, if kept at home, would need services of nurses, physical therapists, occupational therapists, speech therapists, and home health aides. If all were required, the costs would be 50 percent higher than those of the day hospital. This bare-bone delineation of cost would not include the hot meal at noon, the socialization, or the family relief.

Day hospital results seem to be positive and replicable. According to one staff member, ". . . our experience to date indicates that a day hospital within a rehabilitation center is an effective and viable community health care option for older adults. It provides comprehensive, coordinated services which do not duplicate, but reinforce existing health care resources."[17]

Who might go to a day hospital? What about Lewis Hamilton? He is as firmly implanted in the red-brick two-story home on the knoll as the giant oak in his front yard. Move? Indeed no. He wants to stay in *his* home where he and Charlotte moved and reared children and grew old together. Without Charlotte the house is vast as a tomb, but the memories hide, like little animals, in the closets and desk drawers and in the kitchen cabinets. Everywhere reminders of other days keep Lewis aware of the days which used to rush like a clear waterfall over the sturdy rock of his life.

Though Lewis is in danger in his own home, his children's pleadings cannot make him move away. His daughter Hilda flies in from her own home at least every month, and his son Bart calls on Sunday afternoons. They would bring Lewis to their cities or would help him move to an apartment. But Lewis's one-time strength has now turned into irrational stubbornness, and he will not be moved.

The stroke a year ago has left Lewis with many weaknesses which he tries to hide. He breaks plates (including Charlotte's favorite platter with the bluebirds on it). He sometimes forgets where he is or where he was going. The weakness on his left side catches him when he tries to move up or down the stairs, and he is frequently dizzy and in danger of falling. He never reveals to Hilda or Bart that one night he spent six hours on the floor of the study because of a fall which left him confused and hurting to the point that he could not get up and make it in to bed.

It was Bart who heard of the day hospital just opened in

Lewis's town, and it was Hilda who was able to persuade Lewis that such a facility would be therapeutic for the whole family. Gruffly Lewis took the news, his hostile attitude covering his own emotions of fear and fright over the growing weakness and his inability to maintain himself alone and at home.

The physical therapy, medical attention, and companionship work together to help Lewis remain an independent and proud householder for additional years of his life.

Mildred Willis might never have known a day hospital existed if that nice social worker at the free clinic had not told her about it. And where would Mildred have gone then? Into the nursing home where she would have had to room with a stranger and would have had to leave her little garden? The squash were so firm this year, and the peach trees were hanging low with fruit.

How could she go away from this little house that she had paid on month after month after month from the money she got cleaning the Mills Bank Building downtown? Every week, as soon as she got her check, she walked into the same bank and put enough in to pay on her house. And now it was all hers, even if the back steps were getting splintery and the taxes were cutting into her grocery money.

Still she could manage—or at least had been able to up to now. Who would have thought that the diabetes the clinic doctor had been telling her about all those years would get so bad? Who would have thought that she, Mildred Willis, who used to be able to dance all night and still get herself to work, would not even be able to walk?

She looked down at the stump which had once been a leg, and she put her head down on the shiny walker and burst into a crying spell as noisy as a child's. They'd take her away now. She'd never be able to stay in her little house with the overstuffed couch and the bedroom furniture she had painted.

For Mildred the day hospital proved to be salvation. Not only did she get transported there three days a week, but when she got there, she learned how to manage the walker and how to do lots of things without having two legs to stand on. The doctor helped her learn, really learn, the kind of care she needed to give herself and the diet she had to follow in order to keep that diabetes under control. Mildred even manages to keep up her garden, and she's thinking of canning some of the peaches and giving jars of them to the nurses and others who teach her how to live despite her problems.

Is the day care concept successful? How does one measure success? Statistically, it is possible to chart any program in terms of numbers of participants, activities, and cost effectiveness. However, the subtle effects have been stated as follows by one director:

It is our belief that no one really knows what has been successful and just what has failed in the Elderly Day Care program. Only yesterday a . . . man, new at the Center, remarked as he left, "This has been the happiest day of my life!" To others it seemed quite uneventful . . . this particular day he had met people who allowed him to talk, who asked questions, who seemed to care about what he had to say.

Who knows what success we have had? The look on their faces from day to day, their appetites, their desire to bare their souls at times when they are longing for a friend in whom they can confide, their love for each other that has grown from coolness and often distrust to a comradeship that is truly sincere—these prove more . . . than anything what we have done.[18]

CHAPTER THREE

Home Health Services

Home health services in the past have had high ratings but low utilization. The concept of care at home rather than in an expensive and often impersonal facility has appealed to many. The current trend of many young couples to have their infants at home may indicate a reversal of the chrome-and-glass hospital concept so popular for years.

Historically, home health care was prevalent in foreign countries long before it took hold in America. The first such organization was founded in Frankfurt, Germany, in 1892, followed by a similar group in London in 1897. Most countries which have adopted patterns of home health care have followed the British system. Almost 80 percent of the British helpers, now numbering around 70,000, serve the older population. The way in which responsibilities are divided may differ from country to country, but the primary concern is the quality of care and the attitude and ability of the health aide.

Home health care may be organized in a number of ways —as a voluntary agency like the Visiting Nurse Association, a profit-making company, or an extension of a public health department. The most effective programs have connections with health departments, enabling them to give a broad range of services.

Some of the services included in a good home health care program are: home visits by physicians, visiting nurse and social work services, medical equipment supply, transportation for medical needs, and a nutritious food program. All of this sounds complicated until one realizes that a selection of services is probably needed at any one time by any one patient and that home health care has been shown in many instances to bring down the cost of medical treatment. Although home health care may not be less costly than institutional care, it very often provides for better care and faster recoveries of patients.

Communities undertaking home health care must exhibit both flexibility and willingness to change directions whenever the need arises. Agencies with a complement of home health care personnel need to maintain a strong professional staff and recruit and train nonprofessionals. Since patients' needs change, often from week to week, nonprofessional personnel need to have the judgment and ability to evaluate carefully the persons they serve. Unfortunately, because funding for home health services has been uncertain, many agencies have been reluctant to undertake the training and maintenance of a cadre of personnel. One suggested remedy:

If the provision of home health care were to be assigned a valid place in the range of services provided to the older patient and to the medically needy in our system, it is obvious that a more realistic approach would be necessary. Such an approach would be in the direction of establishing broad but basic standards for agencies, and such standards might allow for flexibility in the determination of need and the measures necessary to meet that need.[1]

Fred Atherton thought that life was over after he had a heart attack. Even when he was out of danger and knew that he would live, he felt that nothing was left to make the days worthwhile. Without his work (the doctor said he could not go back to his Saturday selling job), he was adrift. Worse than that, he knew he'd have to move to a nursing home. When Marilyn came out to Oklahoma from New Jersey while he was in the hospital, she said, "Dad, now you're going to have to mind us. We worry about you, living all alone in that big apartment. It's not as if you had Mom here to do for you. You're just not going to be able to keep on like you've been doing . . ."

Too weak to argue, Fred had listened to Marilyn and told her he'd call her before he left the hospital. He didn't get better for days, and the doctor could read the depression and lack of caring in Fred's face. But it was a neighbor, that nice Mavis White, who found out about home health aides and gathered up a batch of information to take to Fred.

After that, he was able to muster strength and work on being better. Knowing that he could stay in the apartment gave him zest. With some nursing care and some household help, Fred would be able to live as he had been doing, to be near his neighbors and the park down the block, and to sleep in the bedroom which he and Frances had shared for so many years.

Fred was fortunate to live in a city where the home health aide program worked. For him it was a rescue mission as dramatic as any emergency treatment.

Who Can Benefit?

A study completed for the New School for Social Research in New York stated that one out of three nursing home residents could be returned to their homes with the aid of adequate home services. Those numbers are impressive.[2] Yet the implementation of home health care has been slow in the United States. Before Medicare was enacted in 1966 only 100 out of 7,000 hospitals had developed coordinated home health services.

The Health Maintenance Organization is cited by hospital administrator David A. Gee as one possible vehicle for providing good care at home. He points out the barriers to home health care as being economic, with hospital care reimbursable and home care most frequently not; physician resistance to making home visits; a reluctance of hospital trustees to risk lowering the daily hospital census; and the hospital administrator's unwillingness to dilute hospital care.[3]

One objective which Mr. Gee notes as vital is a comprehensive and coordinated approach. He underscores the importance of team operation and a planned program for the patient. To be most effective, home care cannot be regarded as one step in a continuum of services beginning with inpatient hospitalization and moving on to the outpatient clinic.

Rather, it should provide satisfactory substitute care in place of inpatient offering. Home care requires proper use of health manpower resources, especially paramedical services. Paramedics can often treat a patient effectively under the physician's supervision while saving him or her numerous house calls.

The need for supplementary help for the client and the family can be seen in the fact that family members provided help in 75 percent of cases for patients discharged from institutions for the chronically ill into their own homes. However, the longer families had to carry on without supplemental help, the sooner they were exhausted and had to call upon the institutions to take the older person back.

Supplemental health requirements are seldom full-time. Estimates by the Levinson Policy Institute show that help can be given adequately about 10 hours per week in cases where older persons have family or friends to assist.

In decisions about home care, the family has to be considered. If the patient is living with an elderly spouse, that person may not be able to give necessary continuous care. Or if the patient resides with his or her children, they may be unable or unwilling to provide the kind of nursing service called for between visits by the home health team. The family structure may be strained greatly by the addition of an older person, often ill and not always cooperative.

Before a home care program is undertaken, it would probably be wise to interview and counsel the family, especially the primary caregiver. The most successful home health care programs have provided training and emotional support for families so they will feel competent and willing to care for the older person.

As has been demonstrated, home services can work only when family support is available. For Marcus Hightower and his wife, Paula, other ways had to be found—but only after a painful attempt to adjust to the home model.

Marcus, who was then 83, suffered a fall going down the back stairs one rainy morning. Paula didn't find him for more than an hour because she had been in another part of the house and, with the television going, did not hear him calling to her. By the time Paula summoned help from neighbors and Marcus was in a hospital, he was suffering from pneumonia in addition to his broken hip.

When he left the hospital some weeks later, Paula assured the doctors that she would be able to care for Marcus and look after his needs, as she had done for the 60 years they had been married. Home health care was set up, with nursing attention for Marcus several times a week and some household help for Paula in between.

No one could have forseen that Marcus, always so self-sufficient, would now become fearful and dependent. He waked Paula three or four times a night; he refused to try the walker unless encouraged and held by Paula; and he demanded special foods and services until at last it was Paula who collapsed and had to be hospitalized.

Everyone in touch with Marcus was appalled that they had not seen the strain Paula had endured. Intermediate nursing services for Marcus could have, in this case, been cost effective and person saving.

The question of home health care versus nursing home care cannot be answered unilaterally. In some cases, home health care is infinitely better; in others, the institution can provide more and finer services and give relief to family members caring for the ill person. But the need for finding ways of providing alternative care for persons with impairments has been well documented. Although figures vary, estimates indicate that at least one out of four people in nursing homes would not need to be there if alternative services were provided in their homes or communities. When one considers that the average life expectancy for persons entering nursing homes is 15 months, one suspects that poor health may not be the primary cause of death. Neglect and isolation may be major factors.

Other patterns are possible for home care teams. For example, they may be available in neighborhood health centers and from those vantage points make calls at apartment complexes. The team can also give care to certain patients in nursing homes.

The variety of services is bounded only by the imagination,

willingness, and resolve of persons developing innovative service delivery in areas where such care has not previously been available.[4] The barriers keeping home health care from being a recognized, usable form of health service delivery are relatively small compared with the benefits to a large population if such services are available.

What About Costs?

What about the financial benefits of home health care? First, if done on a preventive basis, it may well postpone or negate the need for long-term, expensive care. Chronic illness is a fact of life for many people 65 and over, but more than 80 percent of the noninstitutionalized population are mobile. Because mobility is not affected, they are generally ineligible for health care benefits under either Medicare or Medicaid.[5]

The complexity of trying to untangle the various arrangements of Medicare and Medicaid payments, explains Herbert Semmel, often moves physicians to send patients to nursing homes rather than work out payment methods for services under the several systems. For example, eligibility requirements under Medicare Parts A and B differ. Part A concerns post-hospital care, with 100 physician visits per year allowed. There are no deductibles or co-insurance. Medicare Part B allows 100 visits per year, and there is a $60 annual deductible. Then there is Medicaid, which has no limitation on the number of visits per year and covers a broader spectrum of home services. However, eligibility requirements are pretty much limited to the poor. The coordination of Medicare benefits would eliminate many of the confusing requirements and provide a uniform basis for payments.

The Medicare requirement that persons receiving benefits be confined to their homes greatly limits those persons 65 and over who suffer chronic conditions, who need medical care, but are mobile. Without the additional benefits that Medicare provides, many will neglect receiving medical services and may, at a later date, be in nursing homes. The limitation which is set to those eligible for skilled nursing services means that those who could use intermediate facilities do not get served. Although a few states do provide home health care services for persons eligible for intermediate care facilities, most of them do not.

Any discussion of costs must take into account the fact that home health care is not necessarily less expensive than institutional care. At a low level of impairment the home health program may be considerably less, but even then many variables need to be considered, such as the living arrangements and other possible caregivers in the home. In the case of severe impairments, the costs of home services rise more proportionately than do the costs of institutional care. Also, in some instances home programs will not be in lieu of institutional care but will be additional help given to people not now receiving any kind of aid at all. Expanded home health programs, in addition, may well supplement or supplant familiar services currently offered.

With well-organized and -supervised home health care services, costs may rise overall. However, many more people may be served more effectively than they have been in the past. And in cases where help supplements services given by an older spouse or family member, mental health benefits may far outweigh the additional cost. The aid may also help postpone or prevent institutional placement for the primary person or the helping member of the family.

One of the possible dangers: if funds are diverted from nursing homes to home health care, there must be safeguards to keep unethical persons from entering the field and skimming off major funds without giving adequate services.[6] Public and private agencies have, to date, provided most of the services in home health care. Expansion will depend on federal funds to help start programs in many states and communities. Medicare and Medicaid payments could be used for loan repayment, and a network of services providing a continuum of care for older people in many areas of the country could be implemented. Leaders have stated publicly that it makes good sense to have Medicaid provide the less costly alternative. Changes in the law and additional means of checking the varied patterns of operation will make new programs workable.

Although the cost effectiveness of home health care is only

one consideration in the thrust toward such services, it is a factor. Some figures show that a person could be taken care of in the community for between a third and a half of what it would cost for institutionalization. Still, those who dream of millions of "saved" dollars through home health care or day care facilities are setting up false hopes. The chief concern here, as it is when looking at the needs of children, is providing the kind of care which will most benefit those needing concerned services.

The cost effectiveness of good home health care programs might be more dramatically spelled out if it were possible to calculate definitively what financial savings are effected in preventive programs.

Inequities in Reimbursement

The increasing need for alternative programs can be seen in government interest in evaluating what exists and requests for more information. One study prepared in 1975 for the Department of Health, Education, and Welfare points out that to date the central issues of cost effectiveness and appropriateness of in-home alternatives compared to institutional care have yet to be addressed in a way that can influence formulation of valid public programs. The study also states that many persons in need of long-term care may be maintained in non-institutional settings and the number of persons who may need such long-term care is not known. Most significantly, the study reported that the extent to which earlier intervention could delay the process leading to institutionalization has not been investigated with any thoroughness.

The findings identified 45 projects which could be classified as alternatives to institutionalization. Day care accounted for 18, home care, 6, service coordination, 13, and another 8 in intermediate housing and evaluation units. Most were in the Northeast. Clients in most day care projects numbered from 20 to 30; in home care, 50 to 100.

The typical project was found to be relatively small. About half its grant funds came from federal agencies. Clientele were mostly low-income and ethnic population groups, and services in the day care and home care projects were mostly health related.[7]

The sparsity to date of such alternative facilities becomes significant when one realizes that nursing homes have proliferated and have become Big Business. In fact, the nursing home bill comes to $7.5 billion, half of which is paid by Medicaid.[8]

One of the major difficulties in implementing comprehensive home health services lies in the reimbursement system. Authorities who have studied the system have recognized the inequities in payment and the current thrust toward institutional care. For example, in fiscal 1973 Medicare paid out only $75 million in home health care benefits, $115 million less than in fiscal 1970. The total for fiscal 1973 came to less than one percent of the total Medicare bill of $12.1 billion.

These figures were given by Senator Edmund S. Muskie at a hearing before the Subcommittee on Health and Long-Term Care. As Senator Muskie put it:

... It is noteworthy that Medicaid now pays about 50 percent of the Nation's $7.5 billion nursing home bill. It makes sense for Medicaid to support less costly alternatives.

This neglect of home health care alternatives is a waste—not only a waste of opportunity of providing health care and maintenance in the home where patients who do not require hospital care can convalesce in familiar and less threatening surroundings ... Part of the problem is caused by the Department of Health, Education, and Welfare, which has failed to clarify terms of reimbursement for varying levels of care. In addition HEW has failed to require more than token compliance with the law. It should be no surprise, therefore, that most States have not developed significant home health programs, and in 15 states such services are limited to expensive professional care only.

That, briefly, is the picture today.[9]

National Policy Needed

The need for a national policy and coordination of laws dealing with home health services becomes apparent when one studies the tangles of national, state, and local policies which often ironically withhold services which might help maintain community living instead of institutional care for older people. Societal fragmentation and modular living have become acceptable, and the idea of institutions as "alternative" modes of life has taken root in large segments of our society. However, increasingly, attention is moving toward the home and the helpful ways people may be aided to stay in their natural setting as long as possible.

The Special Committee on Aging of the United States Senate has directed many of its efforts toward establishing a workable policy for home health services. A report prepared in 1973 states that it is every person's "right" to make full use of his capabilities and to live in his own surroundings. However, the report charges society with the responsibility of providing safeguards to insure basic economic security and the services necessary to promote health, physical and emotional.

The report also underscores the need for a national policy relating to in-home services:

Although the home as a natural site in care has been largely ignored in our service system in favor of extensive development of institutional facilities, it remains an important resource. It must not be considered an "alternative" to institutional care. This concept must be reversed so that the institution becomes the "alternative" to care in the home. . . . The home is the "vital coordinating link" in the planning of services for the individual. The home and family provide support which is essential to personal security. To the extent that this resource is ignored we deprive the care system of a part of its capability.[10]

A national mandate supporting the development and maintenance of the system was requested by the group.

While home health care is recognized as important, one hopes that it not become a rapidly burgeoning industry without safeguards and regulations. The quality is of primary importance. To date funds spent on care at home have been minimal compared with spending for institutional care. For example, in 1975 the estimated breakdown of $118.5 billion spent for medical costs did not even contain a figure for home health care, estimated to be well under $400 million.[11]

The Subcommittee on Health and Long-Term Care, studying the need for home care services, concluded that from two to three million noninstitutionalized aged persons are bedfast, homebound, or have difficulty in getting outdoors without help.[12] The National Association of Home Health Agencies has estimated that home health agencies serve only about 15 percent of the projected national need. These figures seem even more distressing when it is realized that 54 percent of the counties in this country have no Medicare-certified home health agencies.

Five major recommendations on home health care emerged from the 1971 White House Conference on Aging:

1 Such services must be a required benefit in any elderly health and welfare program in which the Federal Government participated financially. In addition, such services must be broadly defined, with flexible eligibility conditions, widely available, and well publicized.
2 Such services must have adequate public funds and be available free, or on a sliding scale of fees, to the recipient or through third party payments.
3 All agencies providing such services must meet nationally established standards.
4 Other related in-home services must be available to coordinate with homemaker and home health aide services.
5 Homemaker and home health aide services must be available as supportive, protective, and preventive services on a flexible basis as needed whether on a continuing supportive basis or for only a temporary period of time.[13]

Home care must obviate construction of additional facilities. If expensive buildings must be planned to carry out home health care, then cost effectiveness is negated and benefits reduced greatly.

In addition, home care must relate to geographic and travel factors. Patients needing home care must be within a half hour's drive of the central providing area. The utilization of manpower is very much reduced when a large part of any day is spent traveling to and from patients' homes.

Finally, home care costs have to be evaluated realistically in the HMO. All comparable costs have to be considered, whether it be in homebound programs or day care. It is unfair and unrealistic to talk of the care given by the health agency or in the day care center as the total cost per client. Institutional figures include the total system—food, shelter, recreation, and nursing care. What the patient pays for room, board, transportation, and ancillary aids is part of the cost of maintenance in the community. Only when realism is applied to comparative data will it be possible to know the actual differences in costs.

Another difficulty which has been pointed out in regard to home health care is that physicians sometimes use it as an added amount of care for private patients, who are kept in the hospital longer than ward patients and then have the advantage of home health services. In other words, ward patients were discharged earlier and were helped for a short time by the home care program, while private patients had longer hospitalization plus the use of Social Security dollars to pay for convalescent help. Again, comparative and total figures would have to be seen in order to gauge the cost effectiveness of such a hospital–home care program.

Since the primary health problems of the aging are not those of acute illness, the use of home health care seems to be an important service. Too often acute care facilities are used because other appropriate facilities do not exist to service older people, particularly those with long-term chronic problems. Families seldom can provide the care, and community services are inadequate in most instances.

However, in truth, home health care facilities have not proved to be capable of providing the full range of help needed. Too often in this country home health care has meant nursing services provided by visiting nurse agencies or under government auspices. The home health services which have been most successful have provided a combination of in-home services and other medical aids. A comprehensive program including visiting nurses, physical therapy, occupational therapy, supportive social services, household maintenance, shopping, and food preparation has been considered successful wherever it has been undertaken. The rationale often heard in this country (in contrast to European countries where the services are greatly utilized) has been that the first priority is for skilled nursing services and then for personal care services. Actually, however, the home health programs could well provide the patient with the same kinds of care given in an institutional setting. Many patients in 24-hour-a-day facilities can manage their personal care but are in need of continuity of health supervision and aid with daily maintenance.

Without the continuity of health supervision and support which good home health care can provide, the patient is not helped sufficiently in the home services and, before long, has to enter a long-term care institution. Good, comprehensive home health services can slow down or postpone institution-alization for larger numbers of older people.

CHAPTER FOUR

Cooperative Housing

A "place of my own" has been everyone's dream. For the small child it might be the corner of a closet, where precious dolls or small cars can be gathered and enjoyed away from the eyes of others. Or, it may be a tree house, enfolding the youngster in its branches. For the adolescent it is the sacred room, where diaries, paperbacks, radios, and television give stimulus and a sense of belonging to the part-child, part-adult seeking identity.

To the old, home may be the last grip on reality and security. Many elderly people fight institutionalization even when their housing is unsatisfactory or unmanageable. If "a man's home is his castle," for the old it is also his sanctuary, refuge, and identity.

Yet, when the person's home is beyond his means or strength to maintain, what can be done? Some imaginative projects have been undertaken. Replicated, they may serve a large population of "frail elderly," whose only other option might be the 24-hour-a-day care facility. In testimony given by Wilma Donahue, it was pointed out that more than three million older persons in the United States today may need help in housing. Of this number, 2.4 million are candidates for residential congregate housing with services. Dr. Donahue added that if such aid is not provided, all of these people may have to resort to nursing homes, 80 percent of them unnecessarily.[1]

The Housing and Urban Development Act of 1970 has encouraged the development of residential settings for older people who need some support to remain in the community. Statutory authority for the program is contained in the 1974

Housing and Community Development Act, and many low-cost housing units for older people have been built. Some 600,000 specially designed units for low-income elderly have been designed and occupied, giving the older residents the pleasures of recreational and other pursuits in addition to the housing itself.

Felicia Romig faces a move into some supportive living pattern. Faces it as she has met every crisis in life—with negativism and self-pity. True, Felicia is alone. Melvin died in his early 50s. There were always just the two of them. Children would have spoiled their careers, and they were never close with extended family.

A handsome woman, Felicia found her worst enemy in her mirror. She couldn't bear the lines making commas around her mouth nor the gray hair nor the loss of muscle tone. She nagged at Melvin and spent most of her salary on cosmetics and clothing.

And then Melvin had the audacity to die and leave her widowed and without funds. She was angry at Melvin and at the world. On Sundays she went to any double feature in town, anything to be away from home and away from herself. Reaching out never occurred to her. During those miserable, inward Sunday afternoons she never once thought of visiting someone in an institution for the mentally retarded, mentally ill, or aged.

Now she is old and half-ill. She looks at retirement hotels or small apartments and cries at fate for leaving her so miserable. She is unlucky, she says. She has no one to look after her. The apartment is too small; the moving is too arduous. Life is unfair, unfair.

If Felicia's eyes were good enough so that she could see herself plainly, like an unretouched photograph, she would view a woman who carries her good looks and her discontent into her 80s. There will be supportive living spaces for Felicia, but there will not be pleasure, and there will be few friends.

She will undoubtedly find some congregate living arrangement, but assuredly she will not like it. The rooms will be too small, the food too tasteless, and the heating too much or too little. No congregate living plan can suit Felicia because she brings to it her own negativism and her anger at life for letting her grow old and poor. Felicia ages as she has lived, angrily and unhappily.

Felicia Romig carries her unpleasant outlook to extremes. However, every person who moves to some other housing arrangement has difficulties in adjustment. How can one walk away from memories and special comforts, from walls hand painted and rugs selected with careful thought? Life compresses one as he grows older; and as a person discards furniture and clothes and long-saved books and magazines, he feels, at the same time, that he is discarding his youth and that part of himself which was young and full of joy.

The move, then—any move—has elements of trauma. The wise planners of congregate housing will take into account the mental health needs of those persons' changing lifestyles. Special emphasis on encouraging, wherever possible, treasured items to be brought from home to the new housing will help make the transition less hurtful.

"Welcome Wagons" of neighbors could be formalized to set up a network of pleasant happenings for the person making the move. Invitations to other apartments, socializing plans, and offers to help with moving tasks might all combine to make a move pleasanter for everyone.

Congregate Housing

The increasing number of older people in our society means larger numbers of people who have been living in low-cost public housing and who now have grown old in those quarters. This population poses a special problem for the supervisors of the living units, who recognize the needs of the frail elderly and must either supply extra services or evict the tenants.

"Congregate housing is one achievable answer to this imminent rise in demand and need," said Dr. Marie McGuire Thompson. "Under the congregate public housing program

local housing authorities can provide residential environments for their tenants who are substantially intact and well
elderly, but whose functional capacities are somewhat limited due to diminished physical or mental energy, impaired
mobility, or special social or economic conditions. This type
of housing resource planning is an alternative to institutional
living when that level or extent of supervision and care is not
required."[2]

The need for many kinds of services and linkages among
service agencies is pointed out by Dr. Thompson, former
commissioner of the U. S. Public Housing Administration,
and more recently housing specialist for the International
Center for Social Gerontology. The coordination of federal,
state, and local support is another vital ingredient to making
this type of program work.

Good congregate housing for older people concerns itself
with the population wishing to remain independent for as
long as possible. It is a residential program with many adjunctive services and aids to help with the physical and mental
health of the older residents.

The need for congregate housing has been recognized
publicly since the first National Conference on Aging in
1950. It was emphasized by President John F. Kennedy in
1963, and it has been underscored in subsequent White
House Conferences on Aging. Although the need was important in earlier years, it becomes imperative at a time of growing numbers of older people and increasing costs.

Some of the early efforts in congregate housing followed
President Kennedy's directive. They were spurred by a for-
mal agreement signed between the Commissioner of Welfare for Health, Education, and Welfare and the Commissioner of the Public Housing Administration, with plans to
support efforts by local housing and welfare agencies.

Some Models

One development in Alma, Georgia, consists of 12
housekeeping units with kitchens and 40 units without them.

A central kitchen provides daily meals, even for those in the housekeeping units who request them. A buddy system ensures that less able older people will have assistance as needed from the more competent.

In Ohio both Toledo and Columbus have provided congregate housing. State support has been given for some of the construction and the operation of the dining services. It also provided for recreational and health-giving staff and guaranteed supportive services for the 40-year financing period of both developments. A homemaker service, housed in the Columbus facility, provides personal care for approximately 50 percent of the population. Without the services of personal help, housekeeping, and foods, at least half the residents would have to go to 24-hour-a-day facilities.

A total community complex characterizes the project in Burwell, Nebraska, where the 20 housekeeping units are part of a congregate living area consisting of a community building with recreation room, living room, and a kitchen for big events. Recreation and craft programs are brought into the development, consisting of 30 one-bedroom units in five brick buildings.

Some congregate patterns which emerged after the initial three mentioned above have varied in form but not in mandate—to help the frail elderly maintain themselves, with help, in a community setting. The dual benefit of housing plus health and recreational aids has meant independence for persons with tenuous holds to community life.

The Council for Jewish Elderly in metropolitan Chicago developed Group Living Homes to provide an integrated and comprehensive network of services for older people. Included were home delivered meals, home services, information and legal counseling, senior activity and nutrition program, and transportation and volunteer activities.

Weinfeld Residence, a group living residence often referred to as an "elderly commune," opened in the spring of 1973. Six one-story townhouses, interconnecting, provide the privacy of individual bedrooms and the social aspects of a common living room and kitchen for two residents, who prepare their own breakfasts but share lunch and dinner in a communal dining room. A small staff helps with heavy chores and cooking, and a live-in staff member stays on the premises at night. In addition, a part-time activities director, dietician, and social worker help keep the program functioning at many levels.

Residents who enter the facility must agree to continue to use the community resources in medical, recreational, educational, and cultural areas. Fees are based on ability to pay.

Another feature of the complex of supportive services is the Temporary Residence Program, also under the aegis of the Council for Jewish Elderly. This housing helps provide respite care when there is stress in the home, for pre- or post-hospitalization, when a caring family goes on vacation, or as temporary shelter for newly arrived elderly, victims of home disaster, or persons needing home repair and a place to stay temporarily. Financial and contract arrangements are carried out by the client, family, and social worker.

The philosophy is perhaps best stated in these words: "The thrust of the system is towards insuring availability of service, accessibility of these services, and flexibility of the entire system with a focus on service to the individual. Each older person is viewed as an independent member of his neighborhood who because of the very nature of aging may, from time to time, need assistance to support him within the community."[3]

In this philosophy of neighborhood development, professional staff encourage the older population to undertake as much responsibility as they are capable of assuming. They often initiate a service and move aside as older people show willingness to assume responsibility.

Varied Patterns

Many patterns of senior citizen housing have emerged in recent years. One interesting project is sponsored in St. Louis under the direction of the Teamsters Joint Council No. 13. The $20 million development contains two residence buildings plus shopping facilities, union offices, and a two-acre park. The nonprofit Council Plaza is financed by the federal government and run by the Teamsters Union.

Participation is the key word in this project. A resident's council, made up of one elected person from each floor, serves as the decision-making and governing body of the building. A constitution and bylaws contain the decided-upon rules. A director of resident services acts initially to help the new resident find friends and facilities. A housing director and counselor aid with simple matters of housing or complex difficulties regarding personal problems, emergency health care, Medicare, and Social Security.

A number of committees are staffed by residents, who may take advantage of all kinds of activities from choral groups to hospitality responsibilities. A "Council House Newsletter" keeps information flowing. Community volunteers bring outside help for groups in need of services.

A partner system gives additional security to residents. Here each person is responsible for one other and reports if the other is not present at lunch or dinner time.

Health and emergency services are also available, and each apartment contains an alarm button to summon help.

Another unique effort has been made in Kansas City, Missouri, where the Institute of Community Studies has set up a group of cooperative living arrangements known as "affiliated houses." Here several people plan a household together, with individual private quarters but with group duties and responsibilities.

An imaginative and supportive arrangement has been tried in Greater Washington under the auspices of the Jewish Council for the Aging. The council rented an apartment and placed in it three older women (who had been carefully screened). The women have their private sleeping quarters but share the dining and social activities. With the help of a homemaker who comes in five days a week and a social worker who helps with problem solving, the pilot program seems to be successful and cost effective. In fact, the council expanded the initial effort by renting five more three-bedroom apartments in the same building. Residents pool their resources, and the council makes up the financial differences between the pooled monies and the actual costs of maintenance.

In Colorado a nonprofit corporation called 1390 Housing, Inc., bought a large house and provided a living situation for six or seven old people. Residents share costs, as well as responsibility for upkeep, and church groups provide transportation and assistance with some of the heavier work in the household.[4]

Still another living pattern is in Bremen Manor, founded by eight congregations of the United Church of Christ in north-central Indiana. Close to 50 older persons live in the manor, which has been converted into singles and couples apartments. Residents prepare two meals a day, and one is provided by the home.

The San Francisco Jewish Home for the Aged sponsors a group housing project in which residents have private rooms rather than apartments in a facility close to the home. A main meal is provided from the home, and residents prepare their other meals. Help is given by a resident manager and several housekeepers who help with serving and cleaning. Another kind of psychological support is the knowledge that the recreational and other facilities of the home are available at any time.

Using imagination and spurred by a shortage of low-cost housing, the New Orleans Council on Aging has set up a free roommate-matching service. Following a style set by young university people, the council serves as a clearinghouse for people who want a place to live and those who have extra space for rent.

These are but a few of many innovative ideas which have been planned and tried on behalf of people growing too elderly to maintain themselves alone. Congregate living arrangements, well designed and carefully supervised, can help alleviate many of the problems suffered by older people, primarily the difficulties of loneliness and alienation.[5]

Perhaps new lifestyles espoused by many of the younger generation could become models for living for older people.

For example, the barter system could work to the benefit of several age groups. Old people attempting to maintain themselves in their own homes might trade off lawn mowing, window washing, or furniture moving for mending, baking, baby sitting, or proofreading, letter-writing or other chores.

A return to simpler living styles could work to the benefit of the older generation. Small gardens (with heavy labor supplied by younger neighbors or relatives) could provide both therapy and nutrition. Car pools could mean transportation to stores and health services. In exchange, older people without cars could pay for gasoline or could, in other personal ways, take on their share of duties as an exchange program.

Neighborhood councils could also serve a helpful function for both the young and old. The councils can accomplish much more than any one family can. Neighborhood associations can work together to preserve the neighborhood environment, by keeping surroundings pleasant or working to prevent undesirable encroachment from urban developments. They can demonstrate collective power and use the pooled strengths of individuals to perform needed tasks to keep the neighborhood viable.

In addition, such clusters of people form a natural social group working to benefit young and old. The return to street parties or picnics, festive open houses on holidays, and spontaneous yard suppers can provide a kind of milieu in which age differences become far less important than they seem in a society of modular living.

The influx of many young people into older neighborhoods may help precipitate a return to neighborhood awareness. The extended family concept may once again be infused into living patterns.

Still another housing arrangement is the residential or retirement hotel. Here again, it is important that people running the facilities have the understanding, knowledge, and skills to work with older people. Generally such hotels provide a low-cost dining area and some recreational facilities. However, very few offer a range of services such as physical and occupational therapy and counseling.

In Winter Park, Florida, a dozen older people joined gether to form a commune in a 27-room mansion. They patterned their living style along the "extended family" model and stated that they wanted to love one another and live together as a family.

Neighbors protested the influx of 12 elderly persons into an area zoned for single units. The circuit judge, Claude Edwards, listened to testimony for six hours and then decided to see the experiment in senior citizen living. The judge, impressed with the concern and cleanliness evidenced in the home, ruled that he did not find the people in violation of the zoning ordinance.

"Share-a-Home" began in 1969 when a then-food consultant for nursing homes, Jim Gillies, decided to see if an alternative living pattern could be instituted for elderly persons who needed supportive living but did not need to be confined in nursing homes. He contracted for an old house with three acres of lakefront land.

The twelve "family" members pay from $225 to $400 a month for room and board, kitchen privileges, and transportation. Payments are pooled in a bank account. For the management Gillies draws $750 a month and his two daughters a total of $400. A staff of ten keeps the place in spotless condition and so far the experiment seems to be working to the benefit of everyone.

Residents range in age from 61 to 94. How health problems will be dealt with will have to be agreed upon among the residents and Gillies. "Share-a-Home" models are probably viable only for the "healthy" older persons who can maintain themselves with assistance and whose greatest difficulty in living outside may lie in the loneliness and isolation they experience.[6]

Another suggested living model is the older persons' cooperative. The design would follow that of cooperative living arrangements on many college campuses and would draw people who could maintain themselves semi-independently and whose temperaments would permit the flexibility and compromise cooperative housing entails.

A manager, someone young enough to do physical maintenance, would be needed. If possible, the manager should also be knowledgeable in group techniques, be able to lead governance discussions, and help resolve possible personality difficulties.

Ideally, this kind of housing model would be located in the center of the community, close to transportation, medical facilities, shopping centers, and recreation.

A unique aspect of this model would be educational and social programs. And a cooperative bank of skills could be developed so that people could swap services with one another. To make the cooperative way more than a comfortable, viable living arrangement, a "life review" method of therapy could be instituted, with consciousness-raising groups meeting for discussions of the problems of aging.

With home health aides servicing the co-op as needed, and a citizen's health clinic on the premises, the older persons would be able to take care of their health needs at early, preventive stages instead of letting their health deteriorate.

Member residents would incorporate formally as a nonprofit organization and would themselves determine many aspects of their daily living. A self-determination mechanism has special benefits for the older person who has lost, in many aspects of his life, the ability to monitor his own living pattern.[7]

Foster home care provides a suitable alternative for older people who cannot maintain themselves independently but still feel most comfortable in a family atmosphere. Often such a person cannot live with his own family because of geography or temperament, but can get along well with a nonrelated family.

Efforts in foster home placement have been made in several areas, including the Benjamin Rose Institute in Cleveland. Expansion of these efforts throughout the country might provide still one more bridge to bind the gap between community and institution.

Studies conducted by Patricia McGovern Nash on age-segregated housing show an interesting phenomenon which has been called a "leveling-out process." The healthier, more competent residents showed declines in areas where the less healthy demonstrated improvements. In other words, the residents tended to become more like each other. The leveling out occurred in almost all areas, including health and friendship patterns and spare-time activities.[8]

The process of "leveling out" was not necessarily considered negative but was explained by Nash as possibly a case of self-selection. In other words, those who began to sense in themselves a decline in function or health may have chosen to move into the housing project in order to lessen their need for self-actualizing and self-maintenance.

Perhaps further research is needed on the "nesting in" process which may become evident in age-segregated housing which encompasses all activities, recreational opportunities, and friendship needs within one structure. It is possible that residents would do better if they sought opportunities for certain kinds of activities outside the residential facility. As the study cited above has shown,[9] the fact that activities were so close at hand meant that residents had much less reason to seek extramural activities. It also showed that the persons with the highest morale were those spending much of their time in organizations outside the building. Good mental health was evidenced also by those who tended to maintain friendships with persons outside.

Obviously, even when needs can be fulfilled within one site or constellation of services, those continuing to reach out into the wider world for fulfillment are likely to maintain a more cheerful and positive outlook than those who are enclosed.

Public Housing

The dilemmas in public housing have been spelled out by Robert Butler in *Why Survive?* He states that nearly one million units of public housing require that persons have incomes of $4,500 to $9,800, which excludes some eight million American families making less. Rents in public housing projects have to cover 85 percent of the general maintenance; and since rents cannot be more than 25 percent of a family's income, the elderly poor are the ones most subject to exclusion or eviction.[10]

Some of the possible solutions to problems of housing for the elderly include rent subsidies, earmarking percentages of new housing for older people, relief via property taxes, and housing rehabilitation programs.

Architects' View

One study attempting a broad view of retirement and older years housing pattern was undertaken in Southern California by an architect who wanted to develop some new design concepts.[11] The study included four nonproft and four proprietary homes covering a wide range—from remodeled facilities to those specially built; from nursing homes to a hotel for the elderly. Whether the building was remodeled or new, the architect felt that too often mental health aspects of housing for older people had been by-passed.

Contemporary architects are involved in far more than providing physical shelter or appealing architectural design for clients. Many concern themselves with the physical and psychological needs of the population using the facilities. One architect said,

... problems stemmed primarily from a non-realization of the needs of the elderly and secondly from a lack of imaginative use of the design elements by the designer and owner. Lighting, color, corridors, and spatial definition were all segments of the design which were consistently of questionable application. Architects and all those involved in design, must begin to concern themselves more with the psychological possibilities of the architectural experience.[12]

The survey points out that in existing housing many stimuli have been muted for the elderly because of the lessening of faculties like sight, hearing, taste, and touch. But they, more than others, need the extra excitement of color and design, of light and warmth, to continue to respond in a healthy manner.

Some imaginative, definitive action by state and local groups will be needed to make the congregate housing concept workable for those needing the service. The revised ruling allowing elderly persons over 60 to use food stamps as payment for prepared meals in noninstitutional settings under certain conditions has helped provide meals for congregate-housing tenants. Local or state support for supplementary services will help make the group living arrangements possible on a firm basis. As noted, the need for these services increases daily:

Without administrative or legislative action at all governmental levels, institutional care facilities will continue to be the final living environment for too many older persons who could maintain an independent lifestyle with a minimum of assistance. Yet there is little doubt that the glaring gap in the housing continuum for some of the older population is the need for a program that is residential in nature, provides community orientation for the occupants, and also provides those supportive services that maintain the resident in this living arrangement despite chronic conditions or frailty. Adding years to life but depriving the elderly of the opportunity to remain active in society to the fullest extent of their capacities creates self-pity, apathy, and despair among many older people. It also robs the community of the presence and contributions of its most experienced citizens. Primarily then, the concept of congregate housing should be seen as the most viable solution to premature reliance on institutional care when that level of medical supervision is not required.[13]

Even when cost effectiveness rather than general mental health is the primary consideration, the congregate living pattern is one to be examined.

CHAPTER FIVE

Nutrition

Ask Hiram Jackson what he remembers most about his boyhood on the farm in Tennessee. Do you know what he'll say? Most likely it will be, "Those Thanksgiving dinners with all the family around that long table. Man! What a sight! I ate 'til my pants button almost popped, and then I ate some more. And when Mom brought in that hot apple pie, steam coming from the top and cheddar cheese melting over it, I found more room and ate some more."

What would Marilyn Wilson answer if you asked her about her early life? She might talk about the dinner parties her parents used to have. Diane Ferris would recall the hot bread her mother baked, and Frank Luttell would recount stories about getting together with the boys and grabbing watermelons from the field and eating them.

Ask just anyone about childhood memories, and the answer is likely to be related to companionship and food—two ingredients which often spell happy interaction to people.

Only—as people grow older, those joys often lessen. Sight and taste and smell acuity may diminish, and all too often loneliness is the table companion rather than some beloved person. Without the strength or satisfaction for preparing special dishes, older people who live alone are all too likely to fall into a pattern of inadequate eating. Whatever is easy to dish out constitutes a meal, whether it be a bowl of cold cereal or some toast and cheese.

In circular fashion lonely people begin to eat poorly. As their eating habits worsen, so does their physical health. And as they grow more listless and malnourished, they are less likely to be motivated to seek other ways of living or of eating. Thus the cycle continues until the older person is too ill to stay in his own home and must go to an institution where meals are prepared and served.

To break this cycle many nutrition programs have been developed for older people. Along with congregate meals, other experiments are being tried and may form still another bridge in the continuum of services to keep old people in semi-independent living.

Since loneliness and malnutrition are two chief enemies of older people, especially the poor elderly, the Title VII Nutrition Program for the Elderly has proved an effective, far-reaching project. In addition to providing nutritious meals, the program encourages socializing and makes available other supportive services.

Eligibility is by age, over 60, but also by income, ability, or psychological need. Some who can afford the meals cannot prepare them because of lack of skill, or limited mobility, or feelings of loneliness. To all these people the prepared meals and companionship may well be boons. Title VII is designed to serve minority and non-English speaking people in proportion to their numbers of eligible persons in the state.

Each state is allotted an amount on a formula basis. The program is administered by the state agency on aging unless some other agency has been so designated and approved.

Participants may pay whatever amount they wish, but those who cannot pay are welcome. Payment or nonpayment information is kept private, and no one is turned away for inability to pay. Ninety percent of the funds may come from federal sources, with 10 percent raised locally in cash or in-kind services. The group is governed by a project council —51 percent of the members must be project participants. Individual site councils may be set up on request.

The meals are served five times a week at least. Each meal must be designed to serve one third of the recommended dietary allowance, and menus must take into account the special needs of the elderly.

In addition to food, the program provides transportation and escort service to and from meal sites, information and referral services, health and welfare counseling services, nutrition education, shopping assistance, and recreation activities. Nutrition education is an important aspect of the program. In addition to providing the daily meals, project directors give nutrition education to help foster good eating habits, describe the relative values of foods, cost effectiveness, and means of making low-cost foods into appealing dishes.

The success of the nutrition programs can be charted by their growth since they began in July 1973. During 1973 and 1974 the Administration on Aging allocated some $98.6 million for the program. In 1975, $123,750,000 was apportioned for the operation of the program through June 30, 1976.

By May of 1975, 665 projects were under way, providing an average of 228,000 hot meals per day at some 4,400 sites. Sixty-seven percent of the meals were served to persons with incomes below the poverty level.

Maria Ramirez can tell you what the program means. There she was, living in the little house she and Ramon had bought and almost paid for during the long years of babies, sicknesses, and work. Now the babies were grown and gone. Ramon was taken by the sickness in his chest, and Maria could no longer work at the school down the road.

The little house was falling into disrepair, and so was she. There was no one to fix the front steps or to replace the broken window where the cold air blew on winter nights. There was no one to help her get to the grocery store or prepare a meal, and now the skin hung loose from her jaw and upper arms, as if the skeleton had shrunk and left her with a cover three sizes too big for her.

Maria was lonely too, lonely with a cold as bitter as the winter wind. And she would have stayed that way perhaps, hungry and malnourished, if the nice woman from the city had not found her and told her about the meals program.

Now Maria is on the porch waiting when the bus comes to her door. She is fed every day, not just with the hot meals, but with laughter and talk, and games and crafts. The bus takes her directly back into the heart of life, and for Maria each day now holds anticipation and fresh delight.

Many variations have made the nutrition program increasingly valuable to the older population. In one site in Texas, for example, it is carried out in an elementary school. Food is prepared by homemaking students, and the dual benefits for both groups make it a model type of endeavor. Other combinations are possible and are in experimental stages at other sites.

Meals-on-Wheels, under the same auspices, has been directed toward those who cannot come to the congregate meal sites. Here again, many have stayed out of institutions because they were able to have a hot meal at least once a day. The persons trained to deliver the meals were also encouraged to bring, along with the food, an attitude of warmth, concern, and helpfulness. For many housebound older people the contact even once a day with some caring person is enough to give form and delight to a day.

The two programs which make nourishing food and companionship possible for elderly people who would otherwise not have either have proved to be useful innovations. However, they exist in too few numbers to reach all the people needing them, especially the rural old people who are removed from the centers and not reached by those delivering Meals-on-Wheels.

What of them? What can be done for the isolated old? Are there ways in which they might be helped to maintain some kind of independence?

Food for the Hard-to-Reach

A cooperative, interdisciplinary venture has evolved from findings developed in the space program and from federal, state, and university mutual programming. The National Aeronautics and Space Administration (NASA), the Governor's Committee on Aging Research Utilization Program, the Lyndon B. Johnson School of Public Affairs at The University of Texas in Austin, the Texas Department of Public Welfare, the Texas Mental Health Mental Retardation office, and the Texas Research Institute of Mental Sciences combined talents in producing and designing meals, delivering them, field testing attitudes and preferences, and screening program participants.

The experiment is primarily for the benefit of older persons removed from community nutrition programs and needing adequate meals. They are persons who are temporarily ill, handicapped, or live in areas where no meal programs exist. The food and packaging system was developed by NASA with four requirements:

1 Recipients need to have the means to heat water and have access to simple kitchen tools.
2 They have to have sufficient vision, mobility, and manual dexterity to deal with unpacking, opening, and preparing meals.
3 They must not be bedridden.
4 They must have sufficient understanding and emotional stability to accept simple instructions and guidance dealing with the home delivered meals.

And what are the meals like? They are planned to offer at least 1/3 of the daily recommended dietary allowance for individuals 51 and over. They come in sealed pouches or small cans. Reconstituted with hot or cold water, the contents become beef stroganoff, creamed chicken, vanilla milkshakes, spaghetti and meat balls, squash pudding, and other attractive, tasty foods. All the food delivered can be reconstituted with ease and provide variety and multiple combinations. Generally a week's supply can be packaged in a single box. Instructions are simple, minimal, and any person with basic ability to read and follow directions can manage to get the meal into edible shape in a matter of minutes.

Do you know what it might be like for old Garrett Hill? He has been alone in that rundown house eight miles off the highway for two years. After Minnie died he refused to come into town, though the Miller family asked him to come rent a room in the back of their house. He just stays in his little place, and almost nobody ever sees him anymore. His car doesn't run any longer, and he couldn't drive it if it did. The mule died too, and there's no animal around. So Garrett keeps a little garden (can't tend much of anything) and eats some of the canned peaches and green beans Minnie left him. His overalls seem bigger every time anyone comes visiting because Garrett is shrinking almost every day.

Suppose those meals could come to Garrett Hill. The box with a week's supply fits into his rural mail box, and he can manage the pouches and little cans and the hot and cold water. Of course this method doesn't do anything about the loneliness, but it sure does help with the hunger. And somehow even having the food come to him in this impersonal way still seems a little like having a person care about whether he eats or not, and life is just a little less isolated.

Garrett Hill thinks this new offering is a good one. In fact, after the first month he got up enough gumption to make it a couple of miles to the Williams's place and hitch a ride with them into town.

Garrett Hill is way out in the country, and that experiment with packaged foods means a lot to him. But Rachel Means is right in town, and she's hungry and needy too. It's not that people want to neglect her. It's just that there aren't any meal programs here in Centerville. Rachel has always been a private person, and probably few people know that she is getting too feeble to fix a meal or too indifferent to buy the food which might help give her some strength and zest.

For Rachel Means, too, this new packaged food, delivered to her door, can provide a way for her to maintain herself without suffering from malnutrition.

The potential for this program of meal delivery has just begun to be tested. Possibilities include delivery by volunteers who can provide the human touch, answer questions, and help with instruction. The project might also include those in urban settings who are isolated from meal sites or unable to reach food sources. Old people may be isolated in many ways—by geography, by health, by lack of motivation.

Two kinds of meal delivery were tested. One gave people in day care programs the NASA meals to take home for weekend use. For those in the Meals-on-Wheels programs, NASA meals were brought on Fridays.

Early results showed that those who received the supplementary diet on weekends were favorably impressed. Also, those receiving alternative care or home health services responded well to the NASA foods. Over 80 percent of the elderly persons said they would like to buy the NASA food in the grocery store if the price compared favorably to food they were accustomed to purchasing. The same response came from those using food stamps, who indicated they would like to use stamps for the NASA foods. Although most indicated they would buy from one to four meals a week, nearly all reported that in case of illness or inability to shop for themselves, they would purchase as many as seven meals a week.[1] Ways of making this project cost effective have been under consideration by the researchers. If the program can be launched on a mass basis, it is possible that the cost can be kept within guidelines set for meals financed under the Older Americans Act. However, it has been pointed out that even if the NASA meals program cannot meet present cost standards (including transportation and administration), it may be feasible because it reaches a population which cannot be served easily by any current methods.

If the use of space technology for the aging can help older people remain in their own environments, it may well prove cost effective. Independence cannot be measured in financial terms. If one wanted to put a price tag on this kind of effort, it would have to be considered against the cost of lengthy institutionalization.

An Innovative Experiment

Another type of program which has met with success has a threefold thrust: it aids nutrition; it provides help against inflation; and it gives responsibility and status to older people who have been depressed. It all began within the Associated YM–YWHAs of Greater New York in response to laments from the elderly that food costs were so high they were having a hard time maintaining adequate diets.

A self-operated food co-op was developed in 1974, planned by senior citizens. It had three goals: (1) selling food at wholesale prices; (2) providing employment and volunteer roles for senior citizens; (3) serving as a model for other centers.

Funds from the Bookdale Foundation helped purchase permanent equipment like a refrigerator showcase, cheese slicer, and storage cabinets.

Investigation showed that the center could qualify as a training place under the Federation Employment and Guidance Services, and on-the-job training was provided for persons having incomes of less than $2,200 or $2,900 (if married). Publicity brought 20 older people to train for "Operation Mainstream." It also attracted persons from other centers and resulted in the establishment of similar food co-ops in various sites.

The psychological effects on persons staffing the project were almost immediately apparent. The new status, work expectations, and attention were obvious morale boosters.[2]

Although the training program and ability to pay staff ceased after some months, the program has continued on a volunteer basis and has been emulated in other locations. This idea could well be copied in smaller communities throughout the country. It could help numerous older people continue to live in their homes and on their own funds.

Some Findings

Ponce de Leon may have started it all, but researchers, physicians, and manufacturers of beauty products and clothing have carried on ever since in trying to offer answers to the question of how to live longer, albeit younger. Some Soviet scientists have found possible clues in a very simple formula. A simple diet, they say, and proper and consistent exercise provide ways to living longer and healthier.

The researchers, V. V. Frolkis and V. V. Bezrukov of the USSR Academy of Medical Sciences, have found that food of the right quality but in reduced quantities seems to prolong the lifespan of white rats. Although the experiments have not been extended to determine the effects on main organs, work capacity, and the mental activity of humans, the experiments seem to offer evidence that longevity may well be affected by food intake.

Another aspect of the Soviet scientists' findings had to do

with drugs such as poly-vitamin complexes, which they feel have a beneficial effect on fat metabolism and functional conditions of nervous, endocrine, and cardiovascular systems. The use of modern preventive medicine is also recommended by the two scientists.

Still another aid to increased life span, the Soviet workers find, is regular exercise. Clinical and physiological research gives positive evidence that inactivity affects the health of older people and contributes to premature aging.

"No tablets or injections will make up for the infractions of the simple rules for a long life—a sensible lifestyle, proper organization of work, diet, and exercise," say the scientists.[3]

The possibilities for providing suitable food programs for older people range from instituting large meal sites, including transportation, socialization, and education, to delivery of meals to single persons living in isolation. Between the two patterns are many variations. Some involve the older people themselves in cooperative buying or cooking of food. Others are modest efforts to provide nutritious meals in churches or schoolhouses.

In some communities restaurants offer support to older persons by making small servings available at reduced prices. Still others give special rates for meals at "non-busy" hours, such as luncheons in the late morning or midafternoon.

Food is intricately tied in most people's minds with happy experiences and loving companions. When interviewed, young runaways state, "A warm bed and a hot meal—those are the two best things in life."

Food is bound closely to health. When food consumption is erratic or inadequate, malnutrition may result. Accompanying malnutrition may be poor health or varied mental problems, either of which can result in institutionalization.

The fact that food becomes a symbol of much more than the satisfaction of hunger can be attested to by Dr. John J. Regan, a psychiatrist who devotes a great amount of his time to the problems of older people. As a consultant to the extended care unit of St. Mary's Hospital in Minneapolis, Dr. Regan helps make staff aware of what loneliness and sensory deprivation mean to older people. In addition, he emphasizes that food service personnel can aid in arousing the sensory awareness of the old by stimulation of all the senses.

In addition to appealing foods, the older people in this facility are surrounded by people who talk with them and who encourage conversation. Dr. Regan says, "Dieticians and food service personnel have a unique opportunity to provide excellent sensory stimulation. Good food stimulates the olfactory, visual, and gustatory senses. Mealtime provides the perfect setting for the social interaction and companionship which is so vital to the elderly person."[4]

Thus, good community food programs are basically bound to any efforts to delay or prevent institutionalization of older persons in our society. More experiments are needed to find ways of reaching old people needing services.

CHAPTER SIX

A Word to You, the Decision Maker

This chapter is addressed to you, the child of a mother or father whose need for assistance, in many aspects of everyday living, seems to increase almost daily. You have struggled with feelings of fatigue, exasperation, guilt, and anger.

You have attempted to handle your own emotions. But the truth is that facing difficulties attendant to aging is like looking over the rim of a deep well. You can see the depths and the murky blackness without knowing how deep or how cold the waters really are. The wavering reflection in the dark water is your own, and you recognize that what you are deciding for your mother or father you are also deciding for yourself.

And there—already—you have fallen into the trap of deciding "for" rather than "with." The trap is one which has caught us all. "Let's decide where Mother should go." '*We'll* have to put Dad in a nursing home right away." Too often we strip away the flesh from our older people and leave only the skeleton of themselves on view.

Perhaps there are two stages in the decision-making process. First, you need to come to terms with your own attitudes toward growing older. It is not easy. In this culture with its youth orientation, "old" has become too often synonymous with "bad." You feel complimented when people say, "My, you don't look your age." You are pleased when younger people seek your company. If you work, you dread retirement. And you devote many of your efforts to "proving" that you can do everything you could do when you were younger.

It will be hard for you to reconcile the needs of your aging parent until you are able to face realistically some of the problems which will undoubtedly come to you as you grow older. A good plan might be to deal with some of the realities and possibilities.

You may be alone. You may well outlive your lifelong companion. Face that fact now. Develop interests, friendships, and concerns which can help you function as a person on your own, no matter what your age.

You may have financial problems. In 1971, 30 percent of the couples over 65 had incomes of $3,000 to $5,000, and 59 percent of single people in that age bracket had incomes of $1,000 to $3,000.[1] The savings you have put away may not carry you through your later years. Investments may shrink; inflation may increase. Again, can you plan a way to modify your needs and to diversify your investments so that you can live in modest but dignified fashion in your later years?

You may be in poor health. Many of the health problems will be manageable, especially if you develop the habit of regular checkups, proper diet, and exercise. Some health difficulties may become chronic, but again, knowing the best ways of managing them may help keep them contained. However, you will need to face the possibility that Medicare or other subsidies will not cover all your costs. Are you at this time willing to invest in insurance programs which will help you through major illnesses or prolonged health care?

If you keep holding to the image of youth, you will lose your ability to enjoy life. Youth is not a panacea, and old age is not defeat. Each is simply one phase of a life continuum. The Serenity Prayer which reads "God, grant me the serenity to accept the things I cannot change, courage to change the things I can, and wisdom to know the difference" might well be followed in the "growing older" years. The serenity to accept the fact of growing older, along with the will to work toward making the years have meaning, joy, and fresh delights can make the difference. The habit of reaching outside yourself is one which will bring rewards to later years.

This, then, is the first step in the decision-making process of what to do about the aging parent for whom you feel responsible. You come to terms with your own future and thus are able to devote your energies toward realistic ideas about your parent.

Now you are ready for phase two.

It is easy to talk of planning "for" parents at the same time that we insist that we will want independence for ourselves in our later years. Maybe it is time to put ourselves in our parents' place—to try to imagine how it must feel to be bossed and moved like helpless children after a lifetime of making decisions and planning for others.

You say that your parent is incapable of making decisions at this stage? You may be right. Perhaps your planning should have begun some months ago when it seemed inevitable that living alone was not going to be possible for long. However, even now you can seek some ameliorative actions. If you feel that a nursing home is the only option open for your parent, talk it over, even if you know your conversation will be forgotten within the hour. Take your mother or father to visit the facility; talk with the caregivers; maybe have a meal with the residents. Go to more than one, and then find out which seems pleasanter to your parent.

Or, if your parent is capable of rational planning, talk over a number of possibilities. If bringing a caregiver into the home or apartment is one alternative, discuss the kind of person who might be most helpful and the tasks that person might do. Give your parent the benefit of every doubt concerning competence in decision making. Evidence that you believe such discussion is possible and that you value the opinion and cherish the needs of your aging parent will be strengthening to the older person. This kind of decision is painful and frightening, and it is easy to turn such emotions into angry lashing out at the nearest person unless efforts are made to help with the transition process.

Once you have been willing to go through the self-search of your own feelings and have also been willing to involve your parent in the decision making about his welfare, you can begin to face, with realism, what possibilities exist.

You have worked out numerous alternatives. The first effort for Mother, who has been living in an efficiency apartment not too far from your job, was to find someone who could be a companion to her for part of the day. Mother has seemed to withdraw more and more into herself, and you suspect that she rarely ate unless someone prepared the food and served it to her. You located a pleasant woman with a car and made arrangements for her to make and serve a noon meal, take Mother out for shopping errands or visiting, and generally keep her company during the afternoon hours.

Or maybe it was Dad, still living in the house he and Mother had while you were growing up. Since Mom died, Dad has moved into one room downstairs, and the place is a mess. He never makes a hot meal—or a bed—and never seems to take a bath. Again, you locate a competent woman who can do the housekeeping and talk with Dad while she works, and you and your spouse try to have Dad over for dinner once or twice a week.

Nice tries. But they may not be enough. The signs become ever more apparent. The support services do not offer enough time to take care of the older person. In the hours when the companion or the housekeeper is not present, bizarre things happen. Mother has trouble staying continent and fails to clean herself up (fastidious Mother, who prided herself on her cleanliness). Or, Dad wanders out of the house at night and fails to find his way back. A pot is left on the stove and almost sets the house on fire. Phone calls are made to acquaintances at three or five in the morning, and the friends begin to complain.

You face the options then. You have to do so. Where shall the old parent be placed?

There is a day care center in your town, and you make arrangements for Mom or Dad to go there. Now the daytime hours are handled well. The older folks respond pretty well. The staff at the center caters to them, sees that they eat, tries to interest them in games or crafts or activities with other people.

For a while that plan works, and you relax a bit.

But then the nighttime and weekend flareups continue.

The landlord complains about Mom, the neighbors about Dad.

What do you do?

You keep thinking of your own growing up days. Grandpa lived with you, didn't he? Or Grandmother? Maybe both. Or Aunt Nellie? Why, Grandma took over your bedroom, and you slept in the little sewing alcove. Grandma took over the kitchen too, and the family catered to her and saw that she didn't burn the house down or put sugar in the salt shakers. If your parents could do it, why not you?

Before the guilt can spread totally through your being, you remember that there was always Willie Mae working in the kitchen for Mom and cleaning up after Grandma or Grandpa. Mom didn't hold down a full-time job either but seemed to be able to get out of the house for bridge or shopping or the library when she wanted. It would be a different story in your house. All of you leave in the morning like cereal shot from guns. The kids don't get home from school until late afternoon, and neither you nor your spouse returns until almost evening. What would happen in your house?

Well, suppose you moved your parent home and then arranged for day care. That seems to be a viable solution. The perfect way to assuage guilt, handle logistics problems, find a decent place for your parent. Bill can give up his room, and you can put a doorway in the hall and let your parent have a private room and bath. Nice. Everyone will adjust. Everyone will work together. You will find new togetherness and unity in the home.

That is the ideal. That is how you would want it to happen. And that is how it might occur in some circumstances.

But wait just a bit before you make that move.

First of all, get some counseling from a knowledgeable person who can help you see your own family continuum, your own feelings, and the dynamics at work in your family. Sure, your own mother and father had their parents in the home. But think hard. Was it joy-producing and guilt-lessening? Put your mind in reverse and let the years erase themselves.

Remember Mother's migraines? They seemed to come on whenever Grandpa was especially obstreperous and started bawling her out. Or what about Dad's ulcer? He seemed to be down with it about every other week after his mother came to live in the same household.

For a moment forget the stereotypes. Forgo the sweet image of gentle Mother sitting in the rocker mending the children's socks. Erase the picture of dear old Dad fashioning doll furniture for the kids and teaching the boys how to dig for worms. Let the picture book drop, and see yourselves, your family, and your Mother or Dad as they are and as they might interact with one another.

You need to know the price you will pay for bringing into your home a parent whose condition may deteriorate rather soon and who may waken you during the night for nursing services. You need to decide whether your family will be strengthened or divided by adding another generation to your household, and you need to make the final plan as a family with all members voting honestly.

In many instances such a plan may be strengthening for everyone. Older people can add many delights and many positive new experiences to a family. Young children can get a sense of life's continuity, and older ones can learn a new sense of caring. However, if, emotionally, the price will be paid in tension, anger, and divisiveness, be honest with yourself and decide that good 24-hour-a-day care will be the best solution.

The costs for keeping a parent at home in this day and this society may be physical, psychological, or financial—or all three. There are few housekeepers to stay with the parent all day, to keep the house, to respond warmly to the needs of the older person, and to do it all for a meager salary.

What might happen? Let's look at Madeline Thomas— lovely, elegant Madeline, tops in her field as a bank executive —highest paid woman in the business. Her husband, Fremont, heads many of the important civic committees and still maintains an amazing sales record in his insurance firm. Beautiful people. Busy, achieving, well off financially.

They've been able to send son Matthew off to Harvard School of Business, and now there are just the two of them in that colonial brick in the hills.

The empty guest wing, all in teal blue and silver, would be perfect for Madeline's mother, who has just been down for a visit from her home in Illinois. Madeline and Fremont see the signs—the paranoia, the forgetfulness, the dizzy spells, and the fabrications. They know that Mrs. Wilson cannot live long so far away from her only daughter, but they cannot endure the thought of putting Mother into a "home."

Madeline helps to close up the Illinois apartment. Fremont finds a wonderful maid for the daytime and a super-sitter on tap for the evenings they want to be away. And everyone is content with the decision—everyone, that is, but Mrs. Wilson, who meets them at the door in the evenings with complaints about being lonely, about being mistreated, about being hungry, about being robbed. And then complaints come from the maid, too. She threatens to quit. Then settles for a large salary increase. Then threatens once more to quit.

Madeline and Fremont talk in the quiet of their bedroom. They are executive people, used to problem solving. Certainly some rational discussion will help them make decisions about how to proceed.

They investigate the private nursing services and decide on a vocational nurse for one shift and two other eight-hour rounds of "sitter" types of people. The cost begins to escalate. Madeline finds that she is less single-minded at work because of the intrusive problems in the home and the too-frequent telephone calls from the maid, the nurse, the sitter, or from Mrs. Wilson herself.

As Mrs. Wilson's condition deteriorates, the support team becomes more and more professional. Increased nursing services are needed. Still Madeline and Fremont cannot agree on institutionalizing Mrs. Wilson. They talk about the situation a lot. In fact, "Mother" becomes the chief agenda item in their discussions. They go out more because home is filled with problems and petulance, and Madeline's guilt feelings increase as her time at home diminishes.

The financial toll cannot be ignored either. Even with their high salaries, the investments, and with Matthew on his own, they begin to discover that their savings are increasingly tapped for special needs. The twice-yearly vacation (one trip to Europe) dwindles. The planned-for new car is replaced by an overhaul of the old Pontiac, and the carpeting in the house undergoes a steam cleaning instead of replacement.

All of that would be bearable if Mrs. Wilson had not become so difficult. Her confusion most often spills out in anger or accusations. Her senility becomes apparent in her withdrawal, and Madeline often wonders if it would really matter to Mother if she were housed elsewhere.

The psychological toll takes overt form when Madeline drives home one Friday evening after an especially exhausting time. The Pontiac stalled on the freeway, and she had to wait an hour in the sun for the garage truck. Now she turns into her driveway and sees the brand new cream and brown Lincoln belonging to the afternoon nurse.

Madeline puts her head on the steering wheel and weeps.

But then there is Dorothy Garrison—Dorothy who is used to caring. First it was the little brothers and sisters, rapidly succeeding one another from diapers to training pants to school clothes. And Dorothy lifting up a weeping boy almost as big as she, burping an infant whose first word was for her.

Dorothy—loving, nursing, caring. Uncomplicated Dorothy. Everyone she touched was warmed by the sunshine of her concern. Even husband Al, big, muscular, tough to outsiders, was subject to her ministrations.

And now it was Mama, confused, difficult, lonely, sometimes hostile. Dorothy and Al brought her into their home, and Dorothy went right on ministering and caring. Even when Mama grew incontinent, Dorothy tended her as she had the brothers and sisters.

There was never a question of placing Mama in an institution, not so long as Dorothy was around and Al did not mind. For Dorothy and Al, home placement was the only answer, and they never questioned their decision even in the last weeks when Mama needed nursing care almost all the time.

Shirley Miller made the same decision Dorothy Garrison

did, but for different reasons. Shirley, unmarried, hard-working, tense, stopped in every evening at Mother's apartment to see that everything was all right. She often brought a meal and ate it with her mother and chatted about the news of the day. But on that Thursday (she would always remember that it was the Thursday she had had to prepare that massive grant proposal), she was so exhausted that she went straight home to her apartment. When a later telephone call to her mother brought no answer, she dashed over to the apartment to find her mother unconscious on the kitchen floor.

From that moment on Shirley took total responsibility for Mother and for her stroke. She stayed in the hospital room 18 hours a day; and when Mother could be dismissed, Shirley quit her job and brought her mother into her own apartment.

Alpha and Omega. The beginning of Mother's new life. The end of Shirley's old one. Mother improved and Shirley degenerated. In six months she aged five years, and the guilt never lessened, never released its sharp hold on her heart.

"Devoted," some of Mother's cronies said of Shirley. "A loving daughter," others wrote.

But those who knew the dynamics of Mother's move recognized the whiplash of guilt which had permanently injured Shirley and which would not be lessened without some knowledgeable help.

In any decision about placement of a loved one (spouse, parent, other relative), the dynamics need to be recognized and dealt with. The statement which has often applied to working mothers can be adapted to children who bring parents into the home for negative, and often unknown, reasons. What counts is not how much time is left over for other pursuits but how much person is left over after taking care of the aging person.

Dorothy Garrison could handle the situation with a minimum of trauma and little distress. Shirley Miller destroyed herself on the pyre of her mother's disability. The equation calls for careful balance. If the parent placed in a daughter's or son's home is happier there than in some other facility, that parent's well-being has to be balanced against what happens in the child's home when the parent comes to live there.

Some children, of course, are self-centered and totally selfish. They are unwilling to forgo any pleasures or comforts for the sake of a needful parent. Others are giving and unselfish. For them the burden of care is not too heavy. However, for many in between—selfish and unselfish—many valid reasons may keep them from trying to house a frail elderly parent.

Each decision must be seen through the prism of many vantage points. It should be made with honesty, with compassion.

Before making a decision based on sentiment, other people's opinions, or guilt, it might be wise to read what authorities in the field have to say about the problem. Dr. Alvin Goldfarb has stated that, contrary to much popular opinion that children are likely to shunt their older people into nursing homes at the first sign of senility or physical difficulties, they are more likely to keep their parents out of an institution for longer than is good for the aged person. He says that the children tend to maintain the parents at home much past the point where they can give them adequate care:

We have confused issues of actual physical care and affectionate and protective feeling. We talk as though the best way to take care of a person in pain is to hug and kiss him rather than to take him to a place where he can get the physical and psychological care he needs.[2]

Dr. Goldfarb adds that the cooperative approach works only for those old people who have the competence to care for and to plan for themselves. Beyond that point other means need to be examined. And he says, "Without social welfare supports to care for the aged, individuals feel angry —with the old for not being independent and self-sufficient, with themselves for not being able easily to integrate caring for them into their life routines, and angry with circumstances when personnel and facilities are inadequate, very expensive, or very hard to obtain."[3]

It might be good to try to deal with guilt feelings realistically and to agonize less about whether or not to bring Mother or Dad into the home and to spend more time examining community resources. It is possible that facilities exist which will give support and protection to the parent while providing for some of the needs for socialization and companionship. All such decisions must be weighed on the scale of the emotional payment any plan will entail.

Nursing homes are often considered as the "final decision" for old people in society. Much concern has been expressed about alternatives to nursing homes, without, at the same time, seeing that nursing homes or homes for the aged might in themselves be a desirable alternative under certain circumstances. As Jerome Kaplan has said,

> ... It is now fashionable—and indeed a major charge—. . . to seek alternatives to nursing home care. This approach suggests to many Americans at least several possible points: first, there are alternatives; next, nursing home care is the "last stop"; further, independent home care is "better" for aged Americans than nursing home care; people prefer to remain in their own homes under all conditions; home care is "cheaper" than nursing home care; and, many people do not have to be in nursing homes . . .
>
> The indicators, based on clinical experience, suggest that the word "alternatives" implies there are other answers to the nursing home or institutional care system. It is suggested here, however, that the word "choices" may be more appropriate than "alternatives." Choices indicate an armamentarium of services which will allow for the proper service selection. Alternatives indicated that other service types could replace the nursing home. The aims should be to keep from being underserviced, overserviced, or misserviced, not to give a negative connotation to nursing home or institutional care based on the image of the lowest level of such care offered. Why not the image on the highest level of such care offered?[4]

All of which, summed up, means for those of you who are seeking a suitable plan for Mother or Dad, that it is important to see the many alternatives which are possible and the combinations of services which may serve to the best interest of the parent—and the younger family.

Once brain damage has set in for the parent and the needs

111 A Word to You, the Decision Maker

he demonstrates are beyond those which loving and filial care can provide, then the institution as a possible and viable alternative needs to be considered positively.

Or, if there is not evidence of brain damage but simply overpowering demands from an old person who may well prove disruptive to family life and the emotional health of family members, then the consequences need to be weighed with realism and genuine truth concerning personal feelings and abilities.

In any decision-making process concerning an older person, it is important that possible problems be seen with realism and with as much honesty as can be mustered. For the sake of everyone involved, it is better to make a decision honestly than to hide guilt under a blanket of affection or resentment beneath the cover of concern.

Before an older person comes into a home, it is good to examine, openly, the relationships of each family member with the parent figure. If a daughter and mother have battled through decades, it is unlikely that even with the power positions reversed, the two of them will be amicable under the same roof. If the spouse has always been derided by the parent-in-law, that spouse will probably not be able to maintain a loving relationship with the older person in the home. Children too have a big part in such decision making. Although the selfish whims of young people who do not want to give up any freedom or comfort should be by-passed, it is important to see if there are honest feelings which will corrode the family if the older person comes into the home.

Grandparents may often vie with grandchildren for the affection or attention of the parent. And the parent, disturbed by dissension in the family, may lash out at both generations. Such emotional interplay can tear down the family structure, and may be more destructive to everyone, including the grandparent, than placing the older person in an institution.

There is no one solution to the problem of maintaining an older person who cannot live alone. The question is not "home or institution" but rather the quality of care and emotional support possible in either setting.

CHAPTER SEVEN

The Task Before Us

What do we intend to offer as options for the old? Defeat and withdrawal into the island of their solitude? Or acceptance and participation into the community of our lives? If indifference on the part of others spurs the process of institutionalization, then concern can be the chief ingredient toward keeping older people within the community. This concern has to be expressed in action at all levels. Support systems have to be developed in the personal and legal areas. Multiple small packages of services have to be available to offer the frail elderly means of staying as independent and as important as they can.

Attitudinal Changes

Attitudes toward older people might well be exemplified in the story of a speaker addressing a minority group. He continued to talk of a 51st state for them.

Finally, a man rose from the audience and said, "Mr. Speaker, I do not understand you. You keep talking of a 51st state for us. Where would we get the land? How would we get the money?"

The speaker smiled and said, "Sir, you do not understand. This state is a state of the mind. With it you do not need any land. Without it all the money in the world will not do you any good."

Similarly, when we talk of the older population, we are speaking, first of all, of an attitude—an attitude of concern and of caring. With it we shall be able to embrace the older population and bring them into the circle of our lives. Without it, no planned programs will be effective.

Planning will need to be done everywhere—at personal, community, state, and federal levels. It will embrace all areas of life—health, employment, housing, social activities. Imaginative and caring people have been able throughout history to work effectively and imaginatively on behalf of special populations.

Some of the ways in which older people's needs might be met are mentioned in the following pages. Programs which have worked effectively are described, and possibilities through citizen action or through legislative action are delineated. These ideas by no means cover the full spectrum of possibilities, and will be merely a stimulus for others.

Although we talk mostly of alternative possibilities for helping old people live within the community structure, we recognize also that the manner of existence is as vital to well-being as the location.

Perhaps the chief attitudinal change concerns creativity and obsolescence. The creative possibilities of older people have been downgraded in our society, and the concept of obsolescence has been believed. Yet studies demonstrate that learning capacity does not diminish significantly in later years; senility does not occur per se as a person ages; creativity can be and often is generated at any age.

One conference speaker suggested that Erik Erikson's "identity crisis" as part of adolescence had its counterpart in middle life when persons have a second "identity crisis" to discover who they are at that stage of their existence.[1] Other findings have supported the idea that creativity rises in older years, though it may take a form different from that in the young.

A "life review" in later years can be far more than reminiscences over what has been. Instead, it can serve as a gathering in of forces and a mobilizing of energies for those activities which have special meaning. The questions change from "What do you want to be when you grow up?" to "What do I want to do with the remainder of my life?"

Essentially the big push is over—the drive for status or

wealth or special recognition. The quality of partnership or parenthood has been worked out. The demonstration of strength has been made. The compromises and bargains seemingly essential for promotion or other advancement have ended. The clay has been fired in the kiln of life, and now the shaped person can emerge, strong. Beliefs can be expressed; stands taken. The emergent adult can be a force for justice and equality. This role may serve as the most important one an older person can fill.

Some Fantasies

Fantasy has always marked the play of children. Sitting in the scratchy dirt beneath a giant oak or on the curb, skin blistering from summer sun, children huddle together and say, "Let's play like . . . " Or, looking up at clouds suspended like giant balloons in the sky, they challenge one another with, "If you could have any wish you wanted, what would you like?"

Perhaps the art of fantasizing is one which older generations need to develop. In a society where school, work, and retirement are in "modules," perhaps we need to think of whether some patterns ought to be altered; and if so, how that alteration can be done.

Anyone who has been a hospital patient or student or soldier or in any way has had to endure becoming a "number" in some bureaucratic line knows the frustrated feeling of being reduced to computer language as a "thing." One wants to yell out and say, "I am a person. I love classical music; I bake great cheese cakes; I can sell almost anything. I am human. I love and feel and want and hurt. I have a name. I am a one-of-a-kind, not-to-be-duplicated human being. See me!"

Everyone shares those feelings at some times and in some places. However, just as pain is endurable because one knows it will end, so is frustration bearable as we contemplate the very human ways in which we will act when we get home.

But what if the "thing syndrome" were for all times? What if, in the most frightening of the future predictions, we became numbers or robots or subjects? Could we endure such treatment? And if we could, how long would we retain our humanness, our gentleness, our feeling for others? Would callousness, like scar tissue, form over the wound of our tenderness and would we, in a self-fulfilling prophecy, become what we have been regarded as being? How long would it take to fall victim to the belief that we should conform to the regulations of the world and should become less human and more compliant?

It has been said that if one wants to know what kind of culture any society holds, he need only regard the ways in which it treats its old and its infants. The manner of regard with which the powerful treat the powerless becomes the benchmark of a person or a civilization.

By the time a person reaches a point where he needs to be in an institution or requires the all-day services of a day care center, he is generally battered by many crises and resigned to mere existence. If the old person is angry, hostile, or unhappy about the placement, he or she will demonstrate such negative feelings by depression or withdrawal instead of by outbursts or determined activity. Then, just as the studies on learned helplessness have shown, the person who has "given up on life" will no longer participate or attempt to battle. Like the hapless rats in studies on powerlessness, this person will sink to the bottom without making an attempt to swim.

In studies of mentally ill children, experts have found that the acting-out child is often the one who gets attention and who is regarded as being the most needful of care. The too-quiet child who withdraws and who never gives the teacher a moment's trouble may be, internally, as miserable, as ill, and as needful as the acting-out child but is not so regarded by others.

So long as pain is internalized, so long as a person makes no problems for the caregivers, those in charge are often willing to overlook the needs of individuals or fail to give the special attention which might bring them back into life.

How long would we endure in an atmosphere of sterility and indifference? Would we, like the orphans studied by René Spitz, begin to reject life?[2] The infants failed to thrive;

they did not gain the average amount of weight; some of them died. All of this happened in spite of the fact that these babies received adequate nourishment and clean clothes and bedding. All that they lacked was the stimulus of human contact.

If infants can fail when they do not have caring adults to stimulate them; if healthy middle-aged adults would have difficulties enduring inhuman treatment over a period of time; then, what does become of old people who, already confused and ailing, are put into an atmosphere of care without caring?

Let us go back to the children and their fantasies. Let's "play like" we could set up in a day care center or a nursing home with any and all of the facilities imaginable. Where would we start?

Reconstituting generational mixes might be the first step in any of these facilities. The natural flow of life, like a river through a meadow, might be restored. Nursing homes and day care centers would be places for multiple activities from the communities. Since, ideally, they would be located in the center of communities and near bus stops, and since they would be accessible to people from all areas of town, they would attract luncheon clubs, dance classes, adult education programs, and preschool nurseries. (While the fantasy is continuing, it might be necessary to say that nursing homes and day care centers would be small, home-like units built around some common community-use facilities.)

Residents of the nursing home or clients in day care could themselves serve as they are served. Small groups of adequately coping older women might become aides in the nurseries. They could be on duty one morning or five, or one hour or many, depending on their strength and motivation. Some persons might serve as tutors for young people or adults—or as readers for the very young.

A sheltered workshop would attract still other older people who might like to make a bit of extra money doing small jobs for manufacturers or stores. Some of the male residents or clients could teach furniture refinishing or gardening or could make small products for sale.

In order to entice those older people who are already uncertain and "institutionalized," reality orientation would be used constantly. Without guidelines like work or bedtime, many older people become seriously confused about where they are and what day or time it is. Reality orientation keeps them reminded at every turn. Signs on the walls give the facts of the moment about day, time, next meal, and weather conditions. Everyone speaking to the residents calls them by name and makes some personal remark. Everything is done to put the present in context. This kind of reality orientation would go on constantly.

What else would happen in such a day care center or nursing home? There would be visitors—lots of them. Many times the luncheon clubs would meet in the same dining room with the residents, and members would sit at tables with them, bringing news of the town and of the world. Instead of the artificial mixing which goes on during special visitors' days, outsiders would be welcome to drop in for meals and chatting. (These guests would be expected to pay for the food, of course.) Many people would want to join the residents or clients at mealtime because entertainment, short but interest-catching, would become a part of mealtime proceedings.

A library and music room, staffed by people who had enthusiasm and excitement, would be open and inviting. Video tapes would be available for viewing. Exercise classes would be a near-must. Everyone would be expected to stay after breakfast for some exercise training, beginning with breathing and moving on to mobility-training. Small areas would be converted into bars which would open in mid-afternoon for snacks and drinks.

This portion of the fantasy has a basis in reality testing. Dr. Carl Eisdorfer, speaking at a conference at the Center for Continuing Education at the University of Georgia, related the "beer and wine" studies done by Robert Kastenbaum at Cushing State Hospital in Massachusetts. In a hospital devoted primarily to geriatric psychiatric patients Dr. Kastenbaum convinced a ward physician that patients were being tranquilized almost beyond consciousness and that wine might serve as a tranquilizer and also convey a subconscious message of health versus sickness. He arranged for free wine;

and when the wine cart began coming onto the ward at four o'clock every day, patients responded in unexpected fashion. They began to orient themselves in time; they began to change clothes in the afternoon; to groom themselves. The wine study was dropped only when the free wine supply ran out.

The beer study was comparable. Again, free beer was obtained, and one glass was allocated per patient. The beer was served on one of the worst wards, with most of the patients near death. Here too results were dramatic in both the patients and the ward attendants. Almost thirty percent of the patients were able to go back to the "better" wards. Attendants began spending more time with the patients, and the general atmosphere was positive. The beer experiment was halted because of a complaint that serving beer to sick people was not "appropriate."[3]

Results from this study underscore the principle that most people live out a self-fulfilling prophecy. Treated as dependent and helplessly ill, they fall into the sickness pattern. Conversely, given the opportunity to have "well" reactions, they are able to muster coping mechanisms and to respond appropriately.

Mini-buses would be provided (either for a fee or not, depending on the resident's ability to pay), and people would be able to move. Outings would take place almost every day. Some of them might be as simple as rides through town parks. Others might include shopping expeditions in town. Still others could be to motion pictures or plays.

Anyone who has seen a confused and almost nonfunctional old person mobilize himself for special occasions like a family wedding or picnic knows that the residual abilities of persons who seem incapable of doing anything do exist.

Instead of a safe but sterile environment, the fantasized facilities would be places where activities were always going on. And old persons would not be removed from life.

What would it take to make such dreams reality? First of all, intensive training and retraining of staff. Numerous aides would be trained for recreational activities instead of just custodial ones. Administrators would be concerned about the physical *and* mental welfare of the residents and would measure success in terms of human results as well as financial computer printouts.

Our fantasized facility would, of course, have a swimming pool. Victims of crippling diseases like polio and stroke are helped by water therapy. Persons unable to move muscles against the pull of gravity can use those muscles in the water. Paralyzed people can be lowered into heated pools and worked with to try to bring function to seemingly unusable muscles.

In addition to physical benefits, the socialization involved in swimming could also be therapeutic. Almost everyone has memories of recreational swimming, whether in a tank on the farm, a city pool, or a community swimming area. Swimming, picnics, and young delights all intermingle into a kaleidoscope of joyous memories.

For the old exercise would not have to be grim calisthenics. It could be an activity to be anticipated. Simple games like throwing beach balls would help develop muscle tone and coordination.

Swimming or water play appeals to persons of all educational and socioeconomic backgrounds. The water holds universal appeal. For the old, unable to perform many of the physical acts which have been a part of their lifestyle over many years, swimming may bring back feelings of being able to achieve.

Some people who heard of this plan would protest, "But what if some of the old people overdid it? What if their lives were shortened by so much activity?"

The answer might well be that people can succumb as quickly from ennui as from work. People can die when they no longer have anything to live for. Statistics on deaths of those forcibly retired show an extra large percentage of deaths within the first year of retirement.

How one lives can be far more important than how long. Anyone who has watched old people in an institutional setting planted around the "big eye" of the television set knows the withdrawal and isolation they experience. Like people who are near-blind, they discriminate light from dark, movement from stillness, without discerning action or meaning from the programs.

Facilities for old people should not be places to wait for death. They should simply be the most suitable places to spend days or days and nights when the older person has difficulties living alone. To make wax museums out of such institutions is to take from old people the power of personhood.

Even in hospices set up for the terminally ill, the focus is on life, not death. The rigid rules of most hospitals are absent in these innovative settings, where families, including small children, are encouraged to visit at any hour, where patients may have any of their hobbies or favorite possessions with them, and where as many pleasures as possible are built into the plans of every day. If such a plan works for the terminally ill, it could certainly be feasible for those whose chief disability lies in infirmities connected with age and not with some crippling or major illness.

Life is made to be used, not saved. The "miser" who dies with hordes of unused days hidden away within his being has wasted his being, no matter how long he has lived.

What About Costs?

Financially, such a project could be as cost-effective as existing facilities. Legislative regulations would have to be changed to make activity programs mandatory. Many of the changes could be made by adding aides and busdrivers rather than registered nurses. Activity directors would be added to staffs in larger numbers, and they too would undergo significant training in ways of involving even seemingly nonfunctional persons in programs. The interest residents would show would release time for nurses who now spend many hours answering simple complaints from bored old people.

Proprietary nursing homes would probably lessen under these human regulations. But with day care centers added to nursing home facilities, and with Medicare and Medicaid regulations changed to help pay for innovative health delivery services for the old, the total package cost would probably not be significantly greater than the present bill.

Those old persons capable of doing some kinds of work could help in many ways with maintenance. Painting, simple carpentry, mending, table setting—these chores could be rotated and shared.

While we are concerned about where to put old people, our concern has not yet included ways of involving them in their own welfare and their own life activities. Small group councils could help with decision making. Even being able to vote on menus is an act of reality for an old person removed from the decision-making process.

Architects, mental health planners, physicians, nurses, physiotherapists, recreation directors, and others might be enticed in our super-fantasy to take a week off together and come up with a workable model for the kinds of programs which could be developed in every community on behalf of old people. And, of course, older people themselves would be the chief consultants in the planning process.

Some Model Programs

Imaginative, dedicated persons have begun a number of demonstration programs which, on a national level, might be forces in postponing or by-passing institutionalization for many elderly persons. One, described at length before the Subcommittee on Health and Long-Term Care of the U.S. House of Representatives Committee on Aging, is the Minneapolis Age and Opportunity Center. This nonprofit organization offers employment counseling, legal services, emotional counseling, drug, alcoholic, and chemical dependency counseling, transportation, chore services, meals in the home, homemaker and home health aid services, and a nurse when necessary.

Daphne H. Krause, founder and president of the center, met with senior leadership in planning a program of service. Together they coined the word "medi-supportive" to describe the unusual interlocking, much-needed support systems.

Minneapolis Age and Opportunity Center

Decentralized neighborhood clinics make services available to people in all parts of the city. A continuum of care is provided through the Abbott-Northwestern/Minneapolis Age and Opportunity Center/Senior Citizens Clinic where MAO and the hospital, jointly, provide medical, sociological, and specialized services in one setting. Drugs can be obtained from the clinic pharmacy at hospital cost, and a hospital dietitician is available for consultation and education with the older person and/or his family.

Another unique aspect of this center is the Meals in the Community program in conjunction with the Minnesota Restaurant Association. It offers meals at "off peak hours" to senior citizens who qualify and have identification cards from the MAO. The low-cost meals provide the nutritional requirements for older persons and are available to those with low income.

The program also includes "Operation Grandparents." Persons wishing to "adopt" and senior citizens wishing to participate register and are "matched" as requests come in. Also, senior aides help in meaningful ways. Junior League members participate in a variety of volunteer efforts. A food closet gives emergency, supplementary food.

Staff of the Minneapolis Center often become advocates for the person they service. And they have arranged a referral program with the Minneapolis Police Department whereby police refer and coordinate with center personnel when an older person needs help in a crisis. A crisis fund helps tide an older person over the period when he or she may be out of money and needing groceries. A 24-hour emergency service is included. Legal services are available by telephone or in the home. Through the public library, materials are brought to the homebound. Those who cannot get to library facilities can obtain recreational, educational, or informational materials of all kinds.

Funds for the program have been "built" from a number of sources, volunteers being not the least of them. Federal monies for the program have been received through the Community Development Block Grant from the City, through Title III, and through a contract with Hennepin County for Title XX funds. Documentation shows the ways the Home Care Plan has proved to be highly cost effective over institutionalization. In addition, of course, older citizens have been given the freedom to live in the community, knowing that help was available when necessary.

Group therapy and individual counseling are given to families of older persons who are drug-or alcohol-dependent. And weekly supportive group and individual counseling is offered to the older persons themselves who are suffering from alcohol and drug problems. Still another special health component is "Gain Stoppers," where older people who are overweight are put on a basic 1,200-calorie reduction diet and meet weekly to share problems and successes.

A Retired Handyman Project brought together a number of men with skills in various areas of repairs. They now supplement their income by helping other older people who need home repairs.

One delicate component is the Live-in/Live-out Program. Here two groups are served. A person who owns a home but can no longer maintain it fully or well might be able to share it with another person, less impaired, who could take on some of the chores or heavy work and provide companionship and assistance simultaneously. A counterpart is the person who is having difficulty with living costs but who can sustain himself in the community if he can manage some way to keep basic expenses down. These persons might move into the home of a more impaired older person to the mutual benefit of both. Careful, sensitive matching of the personalities and habits of both is essential.

In testimony before the Subcommittee on Health and Long-Term Care, George G. Adamovich, administrator of the Abbott Hospital Division, pointed out the importance of the Minneapolis Center:

. . . Of particular significance is the thrust of this program which attacks effectively the massive problems of the near poor or "corridor" population whose income is above Medical Assistance level and below a level to sustain quality of life. It has freed this group from the harsh reality of choosing between health and food, and, between independent living in the community and institutionalization.[4]

Levinson Institute

Recognition that support services can often help older people maintain themselves in the community has spurred a demonstration project in one community. From the Levinson Gerontological Policy Institute an approach has been suggested to encompass the provision of care and the financing of it.

Because so many older people are brought through major health crises and are kept alive without being able to function independently, the need for supportive maintenance becomes a major concern. Having been aided during an illness of great magnitude, they are now often left to their own resources, which too often means either obtaining help from the family or being placed in an institution. Even when family help is given, the cost in personal energy often means that such aid cannot go on a continuing basis. The ill person then generally is institutionalized.

It is thought that if Medicaid monies could be diverted from simply institutional care and could be brought to help with community aid, many people who are now sent to nursing homes could function in the community.

The approach that would tackle the personal and financial help for older people would begin with Personal Care Organizations, which would come under existing community structure or under some new plan. The PCO, under this plan, would take whatever steps it could to maintain the disabled person in the community. In addition to its staff of helpers, it would subcontract out for other services. Possibly the PCO would serve as advocate for the older person and might help with filling other needs, such as housing, legal assistance, or shopping aid. Day care services might be part of such an arrangement.

Rather than displacing any present agencies, the PCO would work closely with the existing programs. Staff would cooperate with health professionals in obtaining and maintaining health services.

The plan, as visualized, would not consist of the creation of an autonomous master agency. Rather, the community might contain a number of PCO's. Leadership or sponsorship would be undertaken by a variety of agencies and professional groups.

How would financing be provided for these services? This question is crucial to many aids for older people. Even those elderly persons who have planned for their old age via retirement programs or pensions may have enough for bare sustenance with the loss of buying power which inflation has brought about. The person who becomes seriously disabled cannot, generally, afford the kind of personal care service which is needed in order to keep him out of an institution. The revised Medicaid programs, previously mentioned, would be vital. Safeguards could be set up so that those persons so severely disabled that they need 24-hour-a-day care would be placed in institutions and not tax the community service capacity for such intensive help. Those individuals who had sources of income other than Medicaid funds could apply to the PCO's for help and obtain it also.

However, the limitations of depending on Medicaid funds are pointed out by the Levinson Institute, since the insistence that the disabled exhaust all personal resources before being eligible for public care is usually humiliating. Instead, a public program is suggested, or a new personal care benefit within Social Security; and the Institute staff suggests that the benefit could come in the form of vouchers to be exchanged for services or as a cash payment.[5]

The urgent need for long-term care within the community and the necessity for developing personal care services for those persons seriously disabled are addressed in this plan. Such services could provide one means for making older years less isolating and for helping more people who are both sick and elderly find ways of living in dignity in their own settings.

Chelsea-Village Program

Another pilot demonstration of how the homebound aged can be helped to remain in their own areas has been shown in the Chelsea-Village Program in the lower West Side of Manhattan. The three-year study has demonstrated that savings in money can be effected and that many mental health benefits remain for those persons receiving the services.

This particular program began with a search. A team established contact with community organizations, churches and synagogues, police and fire houses, government bureaus, welfare hotel managers, and political organizations. In this way they were able to locate many of the "hidden" needy older people.

Goals were fivefold: 1) to keep people in their own homes and communities, 2) to help such people stay out of institutions, 3) to maintain them in adequate housing, 4) to aid them in staying in the best health possible, and 5) to assist them in keeping at the maximum level of independence.[6]

In this particular program teams of doctors, nurses, and social workers go out from St. Vincent's Hospital. The social workers help the patient in cutting through bureaucracy and finding sources of help other than medical. In addition to the initial team, neighborhood and community organizations are called upon for assistance with homemaker services, friendly visitor programs, telephone reassurance, Meals-on-Wheels, and visiting nurse aids. A nonprofessional staff also assists with coordinating services.

In this area the team has located many older people who were living alone in inadequate, tiny rooms, and whose only "umbilical cord" to life was either a neighbor or a resident of the hotel who would do some kinds of errands. A precipitating crisis such as the death of the helping person left the old man or woman stranded and unable to obtain help. Often the isolation and aloneness made the older person so suspicious that confidence had to be gained over a long period of time before help could be offered.

The financial savings of such a program are demonstrated by the staff reports, which show that in the first three years of service 349 individuals have been referred and 2,110 home visits made.[7] Cost effectiveness is based on the fact that reimbursement rate for Medicaid patients in nursing homes in New York City is more than $800 per month. In this demonstration program the persons are maintained for less than half that amount, and this figure includes the medical costs, housing, food, and other services. Thus, by that calculation, the Medicaid savings in one year came to about $340,000. Further savings are calculated by $150,000 in keeping patients out of acute care hospital beds. Treatment of illnesses at early stages and before deterioration sets in can negate the need for the acute service hospital visit.

The staff report, which delineates the success of this particular program, points out that the complete cooperation of St. Vincent's Hospital, which permits its doctors, nurses, and social workers to take part in the program, has meant that the service could operate effectively. Private philanthropic agencies have aided in the nonmedical aspects of the program.

In order for other communities to have similar programs, the Chelsea staff recommends that adequate payment methods need to be created. The failure of Medicare and Medicaid legislation to provide for medical care outside of hospitals has been one of the negative areas in the ability of agencies to provide good and intensive home health care to those persons in need of such assistance.

Any program such as the Chelsea one, even if financing is adequate, needs the support systems provided by a variety of community services. Many kinds of aid, from personal reassurance and assistance, to physical therapy and recreation programs, are vital to the success of a program geared toward keeping people in homes and communities. Without the rounded social aspects of such a program, the health maintenance is of little value to the old person and his feelings of humanness.

Calling upon all of the combined resources in the community, the Chelsea staff still feels that they have not begun to find numerous isolated patients. In fact, they estimate that they have located only about 10 percent of the people who could benefit from their help.

In reviewing the first 24 months of operation, the Chelsea group reported that of the 245 referrals which had come to them, 222 had had care during the two years. Of these, 23 patients had improved so greatly that they no longer needed the homebound services and were able to live independently. Another 116 were stabilized and continuing to receive care. Forty people were institutionalized in hospitals or nursing homes because their disability was so great that it was impossible to maintain them in a home program. Another 40 died within the first two years, a fact which probably reflected, in addition to their advanced years, the desperate state of the old people's health when they were discovered.

In summarizing the first two years of service, the staff members stated that the financial savings would be enormous if such programs could be adopted nationwide. They call for a shift in priorities. Also, in discussing the hospital-community relations, they state that strong community participation is needed, particularly in finding the people and helping to gain their confidence in the program and in the people administering it. Finally, in talking of the clients themselves, they say,

Health care of aged, isolated, homebound people is a national health issue. These patients can be found, if sought, in all communities. Their requirements for medical services are beginning to be recognized. Professional health workers and government, along with community agencies and individuals, must make deliberate decisions in favor of these people and of the concept of home maintenance. Only in this way will their legitimate call for help be recognized, amidst the many louder voices demanding assistance.[8]

What Might Be Done?

Recognizing the range of community services which are needed in order to give supportive and comprehensive care to older people, authorities in the field of aging recommend the development of models for social delivery systems. One of those authorities, Dr. Robert Havighurst, suggests that such models should have built-in research components to evaluate the outcomes and to provide "feedback loops" to redefine the goals or methods for achieving the goals.

In addition, Dr. Havighurst points out that ways must be found to place the services for older people into some of the comprehensive planning and social delivery systems. He feels that longitudinal studies must be carried out in order to determine parameters and changing definitions of need. As Dr. Havighurst says,

As one reviews the increasing service needs in our society, particularly the increase in numbers of the very young and the very old, and the present shortages in such areas as nursing, social work, and medicine, we must recognize the need to develop at a national level overall strategies for the development and utilization of manpower for services to the elderly.[9]

National Institute on Aging

The National Institute on Aging, signed into existence in May of 1974 and implemented in the Spring of 1976, is devoted to basic research in the biology, psychology, and sociology of aging. As a separate agency with a thrust toward solving some of the problems of aging, it may well be both visible and powerful in effecting action on behalf of older people. Headed by Pulitzer Prize winner Dr. Robert N. Butler, the institute plans include cooperative research with other institutes such as the National Cancer Institute and the National Institute of Mental Health.

National Institute of Mental Health

The need for broad community support systems is well recognized within the important National Institute of Mental Health. Dr. Bertram S. Brown, director of the institute, has written:

Deinstitutionalization encompasses three interrelated processes: 1) prevention of [unnecessary or inappropriate admission] by finding and developing alternative community methods of care; 2) return to the community of all [clients] who have been prepared through programs of rehabilitation . . . to function adequately in appropriate local settings; and 3) establishment and maintenance of a responsive [community] environment which protects human and civil rights and contributes to the expeditious return of individuals to normal community living wherever possible. The success of deinstitutionalization is dependent upon the availability of an array of quality community programs and services.

The National Institute of Mental Health remains committed to the goal of deinstitutionalization when it is defined in these comprehensive terms. We consider it a matter of highest priority to join forces with state and local agencies, public officials, concerned citizens, consumers, and others to assure that all aspects of the process are given full attention and support . . .[10]

Physical and mental health, it has been noted, are not disparate but interwoven. Many of the physical ills of older people in our society may be attributed to their loneliness and depression, just as multitudes of mental problems may result from physical disabilities.

In light of that fact, the statements made by Dr. Brown constitute a vital mandate on behalf of establishment of a national policy on behalf of older people. According to Dr. Brown,

Any effort to develop a national mental health strategy for the elderly must meet criteria set by diverse interest groups. It must be goal-centered, visible, workable, and provide good returns for the dollars expended. While it would require a budget and problems inherent in equitable allocation of resources, it would emphasize program results which could be supported by all.[11]

A national policy, says Dr. Brown, might be directed toward achievement of the following ten goals:

1 Reduce inappropriate institutional care of the elderly by at least 10 percent per year through phasing out the use of congregate, custodial care facilities and phasing in small, individualized social, protective, and health care settings of quality service in the community.

2 Support community projects having mental health relevance and make available to the elderly in their own neighborhoods

and with their participation a broad range of community services.

3 Foster collaboration in service delivery at the consumer level
through political, financial, and personal support of coalition
planning.

4 Work toward elimination of exclusion and discrimination
against the mentally impaired aged in existing and proposed
financing mechanisms, including Medicare, Medicaid, health
maintenance organizations, the categorical aids, revenue
sharing, and the proposed third party payment plans.

5 Contribute to the establishment and achievement of humane
standards of care for older patients through support of nursing
home training and ombudsman programs.

6 Work toward recognition and support of the right to care and
treatment for the aged mentally impaired.

7 Study the barriers to quality care and the obstacles to compliance with standards for dissemination and use in a nationwide
program development.

8 Encourage initiation of additional geriatric programs through
mental health centers of other community mental health
related facilities.

9 Expand the existing number of training places for mental
health manpower serving the elderly.

10 Augment existing support for a broad range of basic and applied research to increase knowledge of the cause, prevention, and treatment of mental disorders in later life and to
provide a better knowledge base for policy decisions affecting
the mental health of the elderly.

A national policy which could give direction toward the
interlacing of services on behalf of older people might serve
to help change the quality of life for persons in all age groups.

National Council on Aging

The spectrum of noninstitutional services desirable for older
people in the community has been outlined in a monograph
prepared by the National Council on the Aging for the Office
of Economic Opportunity. The listing includes health, nutrition, housing, and social services.

Under health services are the variety of home health offerings; neighborhood health centers; medical equipment (such
as needed special appliances); trained sitters both day and

night for post-hospital or cancer patients; day hospitals; night hospitals; laundry service in connection with day hospitals; family allowances for families to care for mentally or physically sick aged at home; transportation to health services; escort services to health facilities; and respite admissions (brief "social" admission to a hospital, nursing home, or other facility during a family crisis or vacation).

The nutrition services include food stamps and surplus commodities; Meals-on-Wheels; lunch clubs and other congregate housing; pickup meals from hospitals or nursing homes; frozen food dinners for pickup from local grocers; nutrition education.

Housing programs should have senior housing (public, private nonprofit, and proprietary); group apartments with caretaking and social systems; home repair services; financial assistance to add safety features in homes; and assistance in moving.

Under social services come a variety of possibilities including information and referral services; legal aid; consumer education; protective services; rental of television, radio, and talking books; telephone for shut-ins; telephone reassurance service; multipurpose senior citizens centers; sheltered workshops; home help of various kinds; homemakers; burial funds; transportation for shopping and social events; vacation trips; multipurpose van; restaurant, drug, and other discounts; advocates for the aged; and outreach services.[12]

Imaginative examples of good alternative care programs have been demonstrated throughout the country. Comprehensive modes of caring for the needs of older people have been developed, and awareness has been generated concerning the necessity for continued patterns of services.

However, multitudes of elderly persons remain confined in institutions because not enough support systems exist to give the kind of care which could help them remain in home or community instead of going to the long-term facility.

One finding reported from the Subcommittee on Health and Long-Term Care of the Select Committee on Aging of the House of Representatives was that, in addition to home care services, outpatient health services on a periodic or regular basis would be an important alternative to institutional placement.

Such outpatient health services should be provided for in clinics which emphasize care of the elderly but are not set up exclusively for such care. "Such care," the report continues, "is less costly than full-time hospital care, nursing home care, and often even home health care, because the center delivers a whole range of services by a variety of providers."[13]

Some other alternatives listed in this committee report include many possibilities which have been examined in this book: the multipurpose senior center; community care organizations, including a package of home health and related services; day care health centers; nursing homes (which should be encouraged to provide alternative day modes); geriatric mobile health units; and annual "health fairs" to give information concerning health education.

Select Committees on Aging

Piecemeal efforts have long characterized services to the elderly. Many laws and practices have been "stitched" like patchwork quilt pieces to existing legislation. Others have been added in overlapping fashion.

The Subcommittee on Health and Long-Term Care of the House of Representatives Select Committee on Aging addressed the problem from the time of its formation in February 1975. Over a period of ten months and contacts with almost 200 persons and 1,000 organizations, the subcommittee delineated the two priority areas in need of greatest attention:

1 The need to correct proliferation and fragmentation of health programs for the elderly on a federal level, both in the Department of Health, Education, and Welfare, and the Congress; and on the state and local levels as well.

2 The need to correct an emphasis on institutionalization in federal statutes and in the Department of HEW, and to establish a comprehensive system of home health and supportive services designed to permit the elderly patient, often inappropriately institutionalized, to remain in the dignity of his own home and community.[14]

The three major recommendations regarding this proliferation and fragmentation which evolved from the committee studies were:

1. Legislation . . . should be enacted to create a system of community long-term care centers to coordinate the provision of health services for older Americans suffering from chronic illness or disability. . . . The long-term care centers would provide local linkage among providers in the otherwise fragmented delivery system and would provide greater flexibility in assigning persons to different care settings.

2. A new House Committee on Health with exclusive jurisdiction over Medicare, Medicaid, national health insurance, health aspects of the Older Americans Act, and health care legislation in general.

3. Legislation to create a comprehensive Home Health Clearinghouse within the Department of Health, Education, and Welfare to gather and disseminate information concerning the various public and private agencies providing home health care and correlative services to the elderly.[15]

Within the area of home health services, the subcommittee made three legislative recommendations. The first was a major reorganization with HEW and the creation of a post of Assistant Secretary for Elderly Health. This new assistant secretary would be charged with coordinating interagency task forces on long-term care, both in the home health area and in institutional care.

The next recommendation consisted of asking for additional appropriations for grants and loans for nonprofit and public home health agencies and for the training of professional and paraprofessional home health personnel. This subcommittee emphasized that home health grants should be appropriated to the full amount and stated that such expenditures would be cost effective in terms of keeping older people in the community structure. Members felt that much of the money should go for training or retraining guidance counselors, social workers, registered nurses, and other geriatric specialists in the home health needs of the elderly. They also stated that such training should emphasize the related sociological, psychological, and supportive needs of the individual.

The third suggestion under home health services was that legislation should be enacted to expand home health benefits under Medicare and Medicaid, providing eligibility to more people in need of health services and allowing additional services as necessary to provide a true comprehensive alternative to often inappropriate and costly full-time institutionalization.[16] The subcommittee believes that the 100 home health visit limits of both Medicare Part B and Part A should be removed and that the two parts should be combined, with no hospitalization required for either. Members felt also that Medicare and Medicaid should be amended to provide mechanisms for preventive health care to insure maximum health maintenance, including a yearly annual physical checkup and diagnostic services. They suggest amendments which would permit professional guidance and counseling for the elderly sick and disabled who are living alone and for the families of the elderly sick and disabled. Another "must" according to committee members is the provision of hearing aids, podiatry, dental care, glasses. They encourage enlisting hospitals to develop outreach programs in the community by reimbursement to accredited hospitals for health and supportive services delivered to the homes of Medicare and Medicaid patients, particularly for post-hospital care.

This subcommittee, in short, has concerned itself with ways of making a continuum of care a reality for the frail elderly in our communities. They suggest a series of demonstration and pilot projects, which would include employing older persons to make friendly visits to ill elderly confined to their homes; instituting a "neighborhood family" where care would be provided by two or more individuals not related to each other; giving families the funds to care for nursing home patients in their homes (with regular monitoring by proper authorities); and making "long-term care vouchers" for approved health goods and services available to disabled persons over 65.

In summary, a consolidation of legislation concerning the needy older person could help to provide a framework for experimental and supportive efforts to keep such old persons community centered and as functional as possible.

The Senate Special Subcommittee on Aging, recognizing many of the problems confronting older people in our society, pointed out that Medicare now covers only about 38 percent of the costs of health care for the aged and that gaps exist in out-of-hospital prescription drugs, eyeglasses, hearing aids, dentures, physical checkups, and other items.

The Committee also discusses the fact that Medicare coverage relies too heavily on hospital care. They say, "In many cases Medicare beneficiaries are hospitalized because effective alternatives to institutionalization are not available. Yet in-home services can be substantially less expensive and more appropriate for the patient's needs."[17]

However, preventive medicine has been proven to be cost effective, perhaps nowhere so noticeably as in medical care for the aging population. For example, while personal health care expenditures increased nearly 15 percent between 1974 and 1975, spending for the aged rose 18 percent during that period, according to the *Social Security Bulletin* of June 1976. In addition, the average health care bill for persons 65 and over in 1975 totaled $1,360, six times that of the average bill of a person under 19 and almost three times the bill for persons 19 to 64. Of this amount, the federal government paid 54 percent of the health care bill for persons 65 and over and only 17 percent for persons 19 to 64.[18]

For the Future

Social planners increasingly concern themselves with changes which will occur several decades ahead rather than in the immediate future. Alterations in the balance of young to old in our society may well result in changing patterns in areas of housing, health, employment, and politics.

What might some of them be?

Concerns about the increasing numbers of older people are expressed by economists as well as by the social scientists. The population of 75 and older is growing at a rate two and a half times the rate of the population as a whole, and the median age of the entire population is expected to jump to

34.8 years within the next 20 to 30 years.

The next few decades may prove to be bonus years for older people, as well as for the very young, but they may be tough on those in the middle years. The reasons may be seen in the baby boom of the mid 1940s to the 1960s, followed by the drastic decline in birth rate. The "boom" babies did not themselves have many—or any—children, a factor which has made demographers shift their predictions from a population of more than 300 million by the year 2000 to an estimate of about 262 million by the end of this century. What will it mean when the dependency ratio, the number of workers per retired persons, drops from 4.6 to 3.5?

Because the base number of the people born in the boom time is so large, the taxes paid by the largest work force in the nation's history should provide adequately and generously for Social Security. Only when those products of the baby boom themselves become elderly will there be a problem of financial provision for a multitude by a few.

Will this trend result in enticements against retirement? There are those who believe that because of the increasing numbers of older people, and the trend toward early retirement, the cost of private pension plans and even Social Security itself may reach some near-impossible levels. It is possible then, that in reverse fashion, older people will be encouraged to stay on jobs, requested to come part-time to their offices, and otherwise enticed to remain in the work force.[19]

Dr. George L. Maddox, director of the Center for the Study of Aging and Human Development at Duke University, believes that pressure in future years will be placed on older people to keep them from retiring in order that they can contribute to Social Security rather than take from it.[20] It has been hypothesized that tensions may well develop between those who have retired and the smaller numbers of people who are working. Political implications may be seen in increased rivalry for offices and candidates from the two age groups favoring one or another viewpoint. Political scientists have interested themselves also in whether or not this increasing age will mean growing conservatism or liberalism. The increasing interest of groups of older people in making collective political statements may increase the potential of the elderly as a political voice in government.

Dr. Maddox feels that two notable "revolutions" are occurring in the aging area during the final years of this century. The first has to do with our images of later life and the unused potential of older persons. The second involves the emergence of advocates and organizations working on behalf of older people.[21] With the elderly constituting an increasing percentage of the population, social planning on behalf of that age group can no longer be considered benevolence so much as survival. Older people who are able to maintain themselves in the community either as productive persons or as people requiring minor support will remove from the younger population many of the burdens, financial and psychological, of "carrying" a whole generation of needful persons.

Thus, planning for older years may be seen as an imperative human ecological thrust, an imperative for the future.

Living styles too are undergoing change. As explained by Roger Revelle, director of the Harvard University Center for Population Studies.

By the year 2000, we're liable to have about 50 percent more women than men over age 65. That's one of the two or three most serious demographic phenomena that we're experiencing in this country at the present time. It makes for great unhappiness, particularly for the women, because men and women need each other just as much at age 70 as they do at age 20, though for different reasons.

Maybe something like polygamy is what's required. Or maybe you'd have to have some kind of communal arrangements where the company of a small number of men can be shared by a large number of women.[22]

The "new styles" in living which have been espoused by many of the younger generation are increasingly apparent among the old, with various types of communal living arrangements in evidence. The segregation of men and women (and even husbands and wives) in nursing homes is seen by many experts as the final indignity of removal of "personhood" from people already suffering from diminution of self in other aspects of their lives. To be human is to be a sexual person at any age, with sexuality defined in terms of a person's concept and being and view of himself in the broader world. The companionable mix of men and women in living and recreational arrangements should have mental health impact on the persons so affected.

Some Options

Options exist for every age group. Two of the most important for older people are where to live and how to live.

The "where" encompasses a range of possibilities which have been discussed. To keep a person centered in his own desired place of living may require minor aids like transportation or delivered meals or occasional house help. Or, it may require a spectrum of services like day care on a continuing basis.

The "where" must be decided upon by "others" who care enough to see that laws and services are oriented on behalf of older people. Most of us are touched by the sight of sea birds which have been contaminated by oil in the waters and who now are unable to fly. Yet, often we are unwilling to see the multitudes of old people who are weighted by the heavy oil of our indifference and who are rooted in the barren sands of lonely living. This indifference must be converted to positive action.

The "how" of living is an individual matter. Most people, unless immobilized by alienation, ill health, or malnutrition, have some control over who they will be and how they will conduct their internal lives. These options of how to live depend in great measure on how one has lived in one's earlier years. Everyone knows an octagenarian whose excitement and zest make him seem young and delightful. By the same token, everyone is aware of the person a half century younger than that who is already "set" into a pattern of routine and boredom. The difference is most often in breadth of interests and attitude toward living.

The most vital ingredient you can bring to your later years, it has been said, is your attitude. Thinking young does not imply fancy hair bleaches or youthful styles in dress but rather cultivating a feeling for fresh thoughts, new experiences, and varied people. The old quip, "My mind is made up; don't confuse me with facts," in reality is not a cause for laughter but for regret. Many people in this society develop an attitude about politics or art or music or people and then, comfortable in their once-made decision, refuse to think of changing from then on. This attitudinal set, which has often been thought characteristic of the old, may be found too often in the young.

The most open option which exists for people growing older (which includes 100 percent of those alive) is that of living as fully as possible. Tunnel vision for life experiences keeps one from seeing all the possible wonders in the periphery of existence and sets one burrowing into the one-way traffic pattern of the everyday and worn lifestyle.

Dr. Martin Buber spoke of two kinds of relationships. One, the "I–It," regards other people as things. But the other, and meaningful, relationship is an "I–Thou," which essentially looks upon another person as being divine. It is to this "I–Thou" relationship that we speak when we talk of attitudes toward any people with special needs, including the old.

The existing options are not for "them" but for "us," no matter what our age. Just as disease or crime or pollution cannot be held to only one side of town, so neglect or our indifference toward any age group cannot be confined to that population segment alone. For we are intertwined in the matrix of our world. We know that the isolation or alienation of the old narrows the boundaries of our own lives. The bell which tolls for them does indeed sound out for us.

And as we become increasingly aware of options possible on behalf of older people, as we endeavor to make those options workable, we enrich our own existence and shine light on our own future. The divinity of the human spirit—at any age—becomes our own.

Notes

Chapter 1

1. Ruth Bennett, "Social Isolation and Isolation Reducing Programs," *Bulletin of the New York Academy of Medicine*, 2nd series, vol. 49, no. 12 (December 1973), p. 1143.

2. Ibid., p. 1162.

3. *Psychiatric News* (September 17, 1975), pp. 24, 26, 27, 31.

4. Nathan Sloate, "Old Age," reprinted by permission from *A Concise Handbook of Community Psychiatry and Community Mental Health*, edited by Leopold Bellak (New York: Grune and Stratton, Inc., 1974), p. 91.

5. Robert J. Havighurst, chairman, "Research and Development Goals in Social Gerontology, A Report of a Special Committee of the Gerontological Society," *The Gerontologist*, vol. 9, no. 4, Part II (Winter 1969), p. 14.

6. "The Elderly in America," *Population Bulletin*, vol. 30, no. 3 (Washington, D.C.: Population Reference Bureau, 1975), p. 5.

7. Ibid., p. 7.

8. U.S. Congress, Senate, *Part 1 Developments in Aging: 1975, and January–May 1976. A Report of the Special Committee on Aging, United States Senate Pursuant to S. Res. 62, July 23, 1975. Resolution Authorizing a Study of the Problems of the Aged and Aging Together with Minority Views*, Report No. 94–998 (94th Congress, 2nd Session), p. xvi.

9. "The Elderly in America," *Population Bulletin*, p. 15.

10. Ibid., p. 16.

Chapter 2

1. Draft Regulations Prepared for Use with Experiments in Day Care Conducted Under Section 222, P.L. 92–603 (Public Law 92–

603, Social Security Amendments of 1972, an act to amend the Social Security Act, and for other purposes, passed during 92nd Congress, 2nd Session, 1972).

2. *Final Report, Adult Day Care in the U. S., A Comparative Study,* prepared for the National Center for Health Services Research, Division of Health Services Evaluation, by TransCentury Corporation, 1789 Columbia Road, N.W., Washington, D.C., under Contract No. HRA 106-74-148 (June 30, 1975), pp. 9–10.

3. Ibid., pp. 139–140.

4. Ibid., pp. 147–148.

5. Ibid., pp. 141–142. (Later analysis shows that third-party payors would save between 22 percent and 50 percent by paying for day care rather than nursing home care. The lower figure represents four days per week of attendance in day care, the higher one, 2.5 days per week. If extra expenses incurred on days not attending, such as rent and food, are taken into consideration, savings drop to 18.5 percent at 2.5 days per week and 2 percent at four days.) Additional information can be obtained from the following: W. G. Weissert, "Two Models of Geriatric Day Care: Findings from a Comparative Study," *The Gerontologist,* vol. 16, no. 5 (October 1976), pp. 420–427, and W. G. Weissert, "Adult Day Care in the United States: Current Research Projects and Survey of 10 Centers," *Public Health Reports* (January 1977).

6. Robert J. Havighurst, chairman, "Research and Development Goals in Social Gerontology, A Report of a Special Committee of the Gerontological Society," *The Gerontologist,* vol. 9, no. 4 (Winter 1969), p. 14.

7. *Adult Day Facilities for Treatment, Health Care, and Related Services,* prepared by Brahna Trager (Washington, D.C.: Government Printing Office, September 1976), p. 21.

8. *Preliminary Analysis of Select Geriatric Day Care Programs* (Rockville, Md.: U.S. Department of Health, Education, and Welfare, Health Resources Administration, Bureau of Health Services Research Division of Long-Term Care, June 1974), p. 52.

9. Ibid., p. 54.

10. From *Aging,* September–October 1972, Nos. 215–216, U.S. Department of Health, Education, and Welfare; Social & Rehabilitation Service; Administration on Aging (Washington D.C.: Government Printing Office).

11. Herbert Shore, "The Day Resident Program," *Professional Nursing Home* (October 1964), pp. 36–37.

12. Eric Pfeiffer, "Designing Systems of Care: The Clinical Perspective," *Alternatives to Institutional Care for Older Americans* (Durham, N.C., Duke University: Center for the Study of Aging and Human Development, 1973), p. 12.

13. *Adult Day Facilities,* prepared by Brahna Trager, p. 23.

14. John U. Thralow and Charles G. Watson, "Remotivation for Geriatric Patients Using Elementary School Students," *The American Journal of Occupational Therapy*, vol. 28, no. 8 (September 1974), pp. 469–473.

15. Abraham Kostick, "A Day Care Program for the Physically and Emotionally Disabled," *The Gerontologist*, vol. 12, no. 2, part 1 (Summer 1972), p. 137.

16. Charlotte M. Hamill, "The Physical Health Care Model of Day Care: The Burke Day Hospital," presented at the National Conference *Daycare for Older Adults: The New Modality*, Durham, N.C., May 19–22, 1976, p. 11.

17. Ibid.

18. Letter from Rene Waterbury, Director of Abilene (Tex.) Day Care Center, to the Hogg Foundation, July 13, 1975.

Chapter 3

1. Brahna Trager, "Home Health Service and Health Insurance," *Medical Care*, vol. 9, no. 1 (January–February 1971), pp. 95–96.

2. Janet Lowe, "The Alternative to Hospitals," *Modern Maturity* (April–May 1976), p. 29.

3. David A. Gee, "HMO Breathes Life into Home Care," *Hospitals* vol. 46 (June 16, 1972), pp. 39–40.

4. Ibid., pp. 39–42.

5. U.S. Congress, House of Representatives, *Home Health Care Services—Alternatives to Institutionalization*, Hearing before the Subcommittee on Health and Long-Term Care of the Select Committee on Aging, statement of Herbert Semmel (94th Congress, 1st Session), June 16, 1975, p. 90.

6. Ibid., p. 100.

7. "Evaluations of Personal Care Organizations and Other In-Home Alternatives to Nursing Home Care for the Elderly and Long-Term Disabled" (Silver Spring, Md.: Applied Management Sciences, 1975), prepared for the Office of the Assistant Secretary for Planning and Evaluation, Department of Health, Education, and Welfare under Contract No. HEW-OS-74-294.

8. U.S. Congress, House of Representatives, *Home Health Care Services—Alternatives to Institutionalization*, Hearing before the Subcommittee on Health and Long-Term Care of the Select Committee on Aging, statement of Senator Edmund S. Muskie (94th Congress, 1st Session), June 16, 1975, p. 2.

9. Ibid., pp. 2–3.

10. U.S. Congress, Senate, *Home Health Services in the United States: A Working Paper on Current Status* (Together with Recommendations and A Summary of Proceedings from a Conference: "In-Home Services: Toward a National Policy," Columbia, Md.,

June 1972), prepared by the Special Committee on Aging (93rd Congress, 1st Session), July 1973, p. 22.

11. U.S. Congress, House of Representatives, Select Committee on Aging, *New Perspectives in Health Care for Older Americans (Recommendations and Policy Directions of the Subcommittee on Health and Long-Term Care)*, (94th Congress, 2nd Session), January 1976, p. 14.

12. Ibid., p. 23.

13. Ibid., p. 25.

Chapter 4

1. U.S. Congress, Senate, *Congregate Housing for Older Adults. Assisted Residential Living Combining Shelter and Services,* a working paper, prepared for use by the Special Committee on Aging (94th Congress, 1st Session), November 1975, p. iv. (This paper was written by Marie McGuire Thompson, Ph.D.)

2. Ibid., p. 2.

3. Ronald Weismehl and Robert Spector, "Serving the Elderly Through the Neighborhood Development Model," paper presented at Annual Meeting of the National Conference of Jewish Communal Service, Grossinger's, New York, June 10, 1975, p. 3.

4. *Newsletter,* vol. 3, no. 5 (Washington, D.C.: National Voluntary Organizations for Independent Living for the Aging, Operation Independence, November–December 1975), pp. 5–6.

5. Ibid., pp. 6, 7, and 8.

6. "Commune of Old," *San Francisco Examiner,* August 20, 1971.

7. From Lynn Manning, "Alternatives in Living for Older Persons," unpublished report (Austin: The University of Texas, December 1974).

8. Patricia McGovern Nash, *Social Adjustment to Housing for the Elderly: A Panel Study,* Columbia University, Ph.D., 1973. (Ann Arbor, Mich.: University Microfilms, A XEROX Company.)

9. Ibid., p. 294.

10. Robert N. Butler, *Why Survive?* (New York: Harper & Row, 1975), pp. 114–115.

11. Hans Proppe, "Housing for the Retired and Aged in Southern California: An Architectural Commentary," *The Gerontologist,* vol. 8, no. 3 (Autumn 1968), pp. 176–179.

12. Ibid., p. 197.

13. *Congregate Housing for Older Adults,* p. 11.

Chapter 5

1. "Meal Systems for the Elderly: Second Progress Report" (Austin: Lyndon B. Johnson School of Public Affairs, May 1976).

2. Allan Greene, "The Senior Citizen Food Co-op: A Self-Help to Cope with Inflation," *Jewish Community Center Program Aids,* vol. 37, no. 3 (New York: National Jewish Welfare Board, Summer 1976), pp. 15, 16, 6.

3. Eugene Sochor, "Good Food But Less—Key to Longevity?" (Paris: *Unesco Features* No. 685/686, 1975), pp. 3, 4.

4. Mary Margaret Lane, "A Psychiatrist Speaks to Dietitians," *Nursing Homes* (April 1972), p. 29.

Chapter 6

1. "The Elderly in America," *Population Bulletin,* vol. 30, no. 3 (Washington, D.C.: Population Reference Bureau, 1975), p. 15.

2. Herbert Shore, "What's New About Alternatives," *The Gerontologist,* vol. 14, no. 1 (February 1974), p. 7.

3. Ibid., p. 7.

4. Jerome Kaplan, editorial, "Alternatives to Nursing Home Care: Fact or Fiction," *The Gerontologist,* vol. 12, no. 2, part 1 (Summer 1972), p. 114.

Chapter 7

1. Grace Polansky, "Age and Creativity," *Successful Aging: A Conference Report* (Durham, N.C.: Duke University, Center for the Study of Aging and Human Development, 1974), p. 110.

2. R. A. Spitz, "Hospitalism," in *The Psychoanalytic Study of the Child,* vol. 1, O. Fenichel et al., eds. (New York: International Universities Press, 1945), pp. 54–74.

3. James A. Thorson, ed., *Action Now for Older Americans Toward Independent Living* (Athens: The University of Georgia Center for Continuing Education, March 22–24, 1972), pp. 48–49.

4. U.S. Congress, House of Representatives, *Innovative Alternatives to Institutionalization (Minneapolis Age & Opportunity Center, Inc.),* Hearing before the Subcommittee on Health and Long-Term Care of the Select Committee on Aging, testimony of George D. Adamovich (94th Congress, 1st Session), July 8, 1975, p. 2.

5. Francis G. Caro, "Organizing and Financing Personal Care Services," a working paper (Waltham, Mass.: Brandeis University, The Florence Heller Graduate School for Advanced Studies in Social Welfare, June 1972), pp. 1-9.

6. Philip W. Brickner et al., "Home Maintenance for the Home-Bound Aged," *The Gerontologist,* vol. 16, no. 1 (1976), p. 26.

7. Philip W. Brickner et al., "The Chelsea-Village Program 3-Year Report January 18, 1973–January 17, 1976, Professional Health Services for Homebound Isolated Abandoned Aged People; A Combined Program of Saint Vincent's Hospital and Medical Center of

New York and The Chelsea and Greenwich Village Communities" (New York: Department of Community Medicine, St. Vincent's Hospital, January 17, 1976), p. 2. (4-Year Report published in 1977.)

8. Brickner, "Home Maintenance," p. 29.

9. Robert J. Havighurst, "Social Services for the Aged and Aging: Suggested Research Priorities," *The Gerontologist,* vol. 9, no. 4 (Winter 1969), p. 61.

10. Bertram S. Brown, M.D., "Deinstitutionalization and Community Support Systems," a statement made at the ADAMHA (Alcohol, Drug Abuse, and Mental Health Administration) Annual Conference of the State and Territorial Alcohol, Drug Abuse, and Mental Health Authorities, November 4, 1975, p. 2.

11. Bertram S. Brown, M.D., "Where Do We Go from Here?" talk at Governor's Conference on Aging, Nashville, Tenn., September 26, 1973, reprinted in the *Congressional Record,* Senate (October 3, 1973).

12. Material cited herein has been excerpted from Technical Assistance Monograph SOS.11, "Developing Day Care for Older People," by Helen Padula, M.S.W., prepared for The Office of Economic Opportunity (1972) by The National Council on the Aging, Inc., 1828 L Street N.W., Washington, D.C. 20036.

13. U.S. Congress, House of Representatives, Select Committee on Aging, *New Perspectives in Health Care for Older Americans* (94th Congress, 2nd Session), January 1976, p. 26.

14. Ibid., p. ix.

15. Ibid., pp. 45, 46, 47.

16. Ibid., pp. 48, 49.

17. U.S. Congress, Senate, *Part 1 Developments in Aging: 1975, and January–May 1976. A Report of the Special Committee on Aging, United States Senate Pursuant to S. Res. 62, July 23, 1975. Resolution Authorizing a Study of the Problems of the Aged and Aging Together with Minority Views,* Report No. 94–998 (94th Congress, 2nd Session), p. 94.

18. Marjorie Smith Mueller and Robert M. Gibson, "Age Differences in Health Care Spending, Fiscal Year 1975," *Social Security Bulletin,* June 1976, pp. 19–21.

19. From *Ford Foundation Letter,* vol. 7, no. 1 (February 16, 1976), p. 1.

20. "A Conversation with George L. Maddox on Aging," adapted from *The Human Condition* radio series produced by the Hogg Foundation for Mental Health and the Longhorn Radio Network, The University of Texas at Austin, 1976, pp. 6–7.

21. From *The Center Report,* vol. 4, no. 3 (Durham, N.C.: Duke University, The Center for the Study of Aging and Human Development, June 1976), p. 2.

22. "Next 25 Years—How Your Life Will Change," a copyrighted article in *U. S. News and World Report* (March 22, 1976), p. 40.

Index